SEAFARERS, MERCHANTS
AND PIRATES
IN THE MIDDLE AGES

SEAFARERS, MERCHANTS AND PIRATES
IN THE MIDDLE AGES

Dirk Meier

Translated by
Angus McGeoch

THE BOYDELL PRESS

Originally published in German as *Seefahrer, Händler und Piraten im Mittelalter*
© Jan Thorbecke Verlag der Schwabenverlag AG, Ostfildern 2004
English edition © The Boydell Press 2006

First published 2006
The Boydell Press, Woodbridge

ISBN 1 84383 237 2

The Boydell Press is an imprint of Boydell & Brewer Ltd
PO Box 9, Woodbridge, Suffolk IP12 3DF, UK
and of Boydell & Brewer Inc.
668 Mt Hope Avenue, Rochester, NY 14620, USA
website: www.boydellandbrewer.com

A CIP catalogue record of this publication is available
from the British Library

BBRA		BCRO	
BASH		BGRE	
BBIN		**BHAR**	
BBIR		BSAN	
BCON		BWHI	

This publication is printed on acid-free paper

English edition designed by Tina Ranft
Printed in China

CONTENTS

PREFACE

Without ships and sailors there could have been no progress and no discoveries – or so it might seem when one considers the maritime culture of northern Europe. From the early Middle Ages, trading settlements on the North Sea and the Baltic were linked by sailing ships. Where land routes, rivers and seaways intersected, there grew up nodes of long-distance trade, such as the Friesian port of Dorestad, on the Lower Rhine, south of modern Utrecht, or the Viking-age Hedeby on the Schlei Fjord in what is now Schleswig-Holstein. The maritime infrastructure was expanded and developed chiefly by an alliance of merchants, the Hanseatic League, whose ships plied the North and Baltic seas.

Drawing on archaeological, geographical and historical research, this book gives examples of how trade and exchange shaped the coastal regions of the North Sea and Baltic, and how from there forays were made along the rivers of Russia as far as the Black Sea, or how sailors setting out from Norway reached the islands of the North Atlantic, and ventured as far as Greenland. My aim is not to provide a complete survey of maritime history, but rather, in the individual chapters, to shed shafts of light on the development of maritime culture in northern Europe from the early to the late Middle Ages, from various viewpoints.

It is chiefly from Scandinavian research that we have learnt to turn our attention from the sea to its shores. As a good example of this I would mention the Centre for Maritime Archaeology, at the Roskilde branch of Denmark's National Museum. In the Netherlands, the archaeology and history of the North Sea is of central importance for the whole nation. Archaeological research into the maritime cultural landscape of northern Germany's coastal regions has been carried out by the German Museum of Shipping (Deutsches Schiffahrtsmuseum) in Bremen, the Institute for Historical Coastal Research (Institut für historische Küstenforschung) in Wilhelmshaven, the state heritage conservation office and archaeological museum (Landesamt für Bodendenkmalpflege und Archäologisches Museum) of Mecklenburg-Vorpommern in north-eastern Germany, the Archäologisches Landesmuseum and state office of archaeology of Schleswig-Holstein, as well as the research unit headed by myself: the Coastal Archaeology Working Group of the West Coast Research and Technology Centre at the Büsum campus of the Christian-Albrecht University, Kiel.

Apart from my own research and lecturing in this subject area, my interest in coasts and shipping goes back to sailing trips in the southern Baltic. I would like particularly to thank friends and colleagues, without whom this book could not have been written. My colleague Dr Christopher Loveluck, now at Nottingham University, guided me around the coasts of the Humber estuary, and Dr Dries Tys introduced me to Flanders. I would like to thank them both. I also wish to thank Dr Anton Englert of the Viking Ship Museum, Roskilde, Denmark, for information about an eighteenth-century shipwreck on the Hedwigenkoog marshes of western Schleswig-Holstein. I am also indebted to Stefan Candrix and to my collaborator of many years, Jens Pauksztat.

Finally, may I thank the Jan Thorbecke Verlag, its managing director, Dr Jörn Laakma, and Dr Uta Korzeniewski, who edited my manuscript.

I dedicate this book to Prof. Dr Guus J. Borger of Amsterdam University, in memory of congenial times spent on the North Sea coast.

Dirk Meier, Wesselburen.

Even in the large sailing ships of the Middle Ages seafaring remained a dangerous undertaking.

INTRODUCTION:
VENTURING ON THE HIGH SEAS

Waves were welling, the warriors saw,
hot with blood …
wondrous monsters … sore beset him; sea-beasts many
tried with fierce tusks to tear his mail.[1]

This stirring battle scene occurs in the Anglo-Saxon epic, *Beowulf*, probably written in the tenth century and describing the eponymous hero's struggle with the mother of the monster Grendel in the depths of the sea. In *Beowulf* the sea is a dark, cold and dangerous element. Accordingly, Beowulf's strength is particularly emphasised, so that he is seen as the 'victor over the sea'. In Nordic mythology, too, the sea is represented as the home of inhuman creatures and monsters, when, for example, the thunder-god Thor attempts to catch the terrifying sea serpent.

In ancient Nordic myth the sea also plays a part in the creation of mankind. The three gods Odin, Hoernir and Lodur were walking along the shore when they came across two tree trunks, probably driftwood. They lifted up the timbers and bestowed on them the form of male and female. So the very first human beings originated beside the sea.

Beowulf, on the other hand, possessed the weapon with which to tame the sea: a magnificent ship. So we read:

In Nordic mythology the sea appears as the abode of monsters.

the men pushed off,
on its willing way, the well-braced craft.
Then moved o'er the waters by might of the wind
that bark like a bird with breast of foam.[2]

---

[1] From '*Beowulf* in Hypertext', to be found on the website of McMaster University, Hamilton, Ontario (www.humanities.mcmaster.ca/~beowulf/)
[2] Ibid.

SHIPS

Only with seaworthy ships could the seas be traversed. The wind can strengthen quickly and turn into a storm, and mountainous waves can build up. Ships with oars or sails were the first to be capable of withstanding these forces of nature; boats propelled by paddle, on the other hand, had only a low freeboard, and the water could easily wash over the gunwale. Such craft were only capable of short journeys close to the shore or along rivers. The tradition of seagoing ships in northern Europe did not develop until the first centuries AD.

Large ships propelled by oars are illustrated on Runic stones from the period between AD 400 and 600 found on the Swedish island of Gotland. These oar-ships, with their characteristic high stems at the bow and stern, their wide hulls and high freeboard, were very seaworthy. What is more, they could be run straight up on to the beach and needed no harbour. It was in ships like this that the Jutes, Angles and Saxons landed in England.

We can be sure that by some time in the second half of the first millennium AD ships were equipped with large sails. Yet even the ships of the Viking period, with their slender shape, were reliant on highly efficient oarsmanship.

SAILING

The people of the Mediterranean world had used the power of sail several centuries earlier than the northern races, and it was only this that made it possible to risk voyages across the open seas. Until the invention of steam power, wind provided the crucial energy for movement on the water. Even so, engine-driven ships have not wholly succeeded in driving out sail. To this day, sailing has a fascination, and sailing craft epitomise our maritime culture.

Someone who boards a yacht with no knowledge of sailing cannot simply switch on and drive off as one would in a motor-boat. Recognising the direction of the wind, assessing its force, setting the sails and steering a course are all skills that have to be learned. When the wind relative to the ship strikes the vessel from astern (or behind) it is said to be 'aft', and it is 'abeam' when roughly at right angles to the ship. The closer one sails to the wind, the 'higher' one is said to be pointing. If you try to turn fully into the wind, the sails flap and the ship comes to a stop. In order to sail against the direction of the wind, you have to tack. This entails hauling the sails taut, and sailing at about 40 degrees to the wind on one side, then 'going about' and sailing at about 40 degrees on the other.

In a modern yacht this can be done without difficulty. Not so in the old sailing ships. The first sailing vessels could really only sail well with the wind aft. It is true that medieval cogs could sail with the wind abeam, but with their square rig they could not point as high – that is, sail at such a narrow angle to the wind – as modern yachts can. This can really only be done with a triangular fore-and-aft sail, the jib, set in front of the mast.

NAVIGATION

Sailing ships did, however, have an inestimable advantage: for the first time man was able to span greater distances across the sea. The earliest voyages still followed coasts and went between islands, so that the sailors were never out of sight of land. This meant that during the day they could find their way by characteristic landmarks such as rocks, bays, promontories, sandbanks, reefs or manmade constructions like church towers. On a rocky coast these are easy to make out, but on a flat coastline like that of the North Sea where the land rises only slightly above the horizon it can be much more difficult.

With the help of these visual navigation techniques the seamen could establish the position of their vessels. The lead-line, simple little tables for measuring the Pole Star's elevation above the horizon, and the solar compass completed the array of technical and navigational aids. Until well into the sixteenth century sailors in northern Europe navigated without charts. There were no schools of navigation, and sea voyages were a matter of experience.

SEAMANSHIP

If navigation was elementary, the early stages of shipbuilding in northern Europe were equally unsophisticated. For a long time, building ships was a matter of trial and error. This makes it difficult for archaeologists to define with certainty the origin of early medieval ships, particularly as there is no written record. Wrecked ships did not end up in the place they were built, but somewhere on their voyage between ports. What makes it even more difficult to assign a ship to a specific shipyard or port is the fact that ships were a transnational mode of transport.

Apart from written historical evidence, we learn much from a ship's cargo manifest about sea routes and conditions in those days. Ships did not, of course, carry only cargo, but also took on board equipment, provisions and crew from various ports. Thus shipwrecks bear valuable

Archaeologists are bringing to light the heritage of the medieval coastal landscape. The photograph shows the landing-stage at Wellinghausen in the Dithmarschen region of western Schleswig-Holstein, a port which, in about AD 700, was linked by a creek to the sea and maritime trade.

witness to the history of daily life, business and culture. They are a part of our cultural heritage – for seafaring had a decisive influence on the economic development of Europe.

THE COASTAL LANDSCAPE AND ITS HARBOURS

Maritime culture in the North Sea and Baltic areas was originally based on purely agrarian societies. Today, on the other hand, the coast is characterised by large port cities and small fishing harbours. The decisive turning-point in the seafaring and coastal history of northern Europe had already taken place, when merchants gave up their land-based pattern of settlement and established themselves in towns that were specifically orientated towards trade. These were situated at the intersections of land, river and sea routes. The coast and its immediate hinterland were linked in variety of ways.

So it was that in northern Europe in the seventh and eighth centuries the foundations were laid for a maritime culture spanning the North Sea and Baltic with various interconnected regions of commerce. At the intersection of sea-borne, coastal and river routes, goods from Byzantium reached northern Europe and thence, from the Friesian (now Dutch and north-west German) coastal areas, onward to England and Scandinavia. Quite a number of the early trading centres around the North and Baltic seas died out, while others grew into cities.

The port cities, as well as the wharves, shipyards, canals, docks and warehouses, are just as much a part of the maritime heritage as are the ships themselves. Harbour facilities include the quays and cranes, and the merchants' storehouses and offices. Special navigation-marks and lighthouses served to make shipping safer. Many of the technical improvements to the maritime infrastructure resulted from peaceable trading. With the demand for more and more goods, larger ships became necessary, which could be more easily loaded and unloaded at wharves, while a crucial advantage of Viking warships was that they could be run up on beaches.

In the early Middle Ages ships usually sailed right up to the shore and were unloaded at 'landings'. To allow ships to float up to 'steep-to' shores (where the land below the surface of the water drops almost vertically), wharves had to be constructed to facilitate unloading. This often entailed building tongue-shaped moles jutting out into the water, or jetties made of wood and stone running parallel to the shore. Wooden jetties and moles for lying alongside already existed in early medieval trading centres such as Hedeby and Wolin. Later, the seaports of the Hansa boasted fixed wharves with all the necessary facilities for loading, unloading and storing cargoes. By then the merchants no longer went to sea themselves, but directed their commerce from permanent offices in the ports.

MERCHANTS AND SEABORNE TRADE

The most important element in a maritime civilisation is the exchange of goods. This became the driving force behind the evolution of seafaring and shaped the face of the coasts. It is important to remember that trade in the Middle Ages did not always mean the same thing as it does today. In addition to the profit-orientated activities of merchants, there were other forms of commerce. Thus loyal subjects presented gifts to their rulers and were rewarded by them with weapons or jewels. The receipt and distribution of gifts was part of the social system. Senior clerics also exchanged gifts, and within the nobility, too, reciprocal gifts played a part. As well as this peaceful exchange of merchandise, property could change ownership in other ways. Through pillage, plunder or the seizure of ships many goods exchanged hands as a result of violence.

Goods were manufactured ashore and traded over long distances by ship, along rivers and coasts and across the sea. The people responsible for this peaceful commerce were the merchants. Beginning in the medieval period, they have left a historical and archaeological record, enabling us to describe accurately the transport of goods by water, as well as the goods themselves, the trading centres, markets and mercantile settlements.

From the early Middle Ages onwards, the expansion of the commercial network became a political and economic task of the first order – and it has remained so to this day. In the areas once occupied by the Romans there were long-distance highways as well as waterways and seaways, but these were now in poor condition, and in the north, in regions settled by Saxons, Friesians, Slavs and Scandinavian Vikings, they did not exist at all. Hence, the transport of goods by ship was of great importance.

Along with the money economy, it was shipping that made long-distance trade possible. Archaeological finds around the North Sea and Baltic prove, for example, that millstones of Rhineland basalt, large jars of Norwegian soapstone (steatite), iron from Sweden, quicksilver from southern Europe, combs and cloths from Friesland, as well as furs and slaves from the east, were being traded, and that in the early Middle Ages huge numbers of Arab

(above) River navigation played an important part in foreign trade.
(below) Sea-borne trade was under constant threat from piracy. The chronicle of Matthew
Paris tells of Eustachius, the black monk, who terrorised the English Channel around 1200.

coins and even silk reached the Baltic region. Without river, coastal and high-sea shipping, none of these goods would have become so widespread.

To judge from the different currencies in circulation, a variety of economic regions were engaged in this trading. At the same time, during the early Middle Ages, barter played a large role in the North Sea and Baltic, even though goods were weighed against precious metals. Silver, weighed and cut into pieces, was a payment medium, but silver coins were sometimes used as well. Therefore, in order to test the soundness of a payment medium, many merchants in northern Europe carried small folding scales with them. The Nordic lands formed a common currency area with the Slav-populated regions around the southern fringe of the Baltic. This was based on a money-by-weight economy and thus differed from southern and western Europe, where a coinage-based economy had already existed for a long time.

THE ORIGIN OF THE SEAFARERS

Who were the various groups who exchanged goods and operated as traders? After the *Völkerwanderung* – the westward European migrations of the early centuries AD – different tribes and peoples settled on the coasts. Friesians

The great All-German Shooting Festival in Hamburg in 1909 included a pageant recalling the supposed sea-power of the Hanseatic League and linking it with Germany's future on the world's oceans. It is well known that Germany's decision to build a powerful navy was one of the causes of the First World War. But Germany's maritime past had not been entirely peaceable either. This scene from the pageant shows the medieval pirate Klaus Störtebeker being taking prisoner.

and Saxons were on the North Sea coast; in the age of migration after the Romans had departed, Saxons, Angles and Jutes reached England by ship and put down roots there. Slavs settled on the southern coast of the Baltic, while Danish, Swedish and Norwegian Vikings made their settlements in Scandinavia. On the southern Baltic coast there lived various Slavic tribes, like the Obodritans in eastern Holstein and western Mecklenburg, or the Pomeranians further east. Still further to the east, there were Baltic and Finno-Ugrian races, today's Latvians, Lithuanians, Estonians and Finns.

In the ninth and tenth centuries, the men of the north, the Norsemen or Vikings, took to the seas in their long-boats, to trade, conquer and maraud: Danish Vikings founded the trading settlement of Hedeby on the Schlei Fjord; and it was Danish and Norwegian Vikings who plundered the coasts of Britain and Ireland. Swedish Vikings chiefly headed east up the rivers into the vast plains of Russia and eventually to Byzantium. It was a lack of good farmland and flight from the increasingly centralised power of the king that drove the Norwegian Vikings to undertake hazardous voyages across the northern seas and the North Atlantic, and finally to reach Iceland and Greenland. Later, other Norsemen, known to history as the Normans, colonised north-western France (Normandy) and even Sicily.

In the course of German colonisation of north-east Europe, German merchants founded trading bases on the southern Baltic coast – and so arose the network of Hanseatic cities. The merchants' ships now sailed between the kingdoms of Norway, Sweden, Denmark and England, as well as the Holy Roman (in fact, German) Empire and the territory of the Teutonic Knights, who were spreading Christianity through the east with fire and sword. At the eastern extremity of the Baltic stood Finland and the Principality of Novgorod. In the Baltic hinterland Lithuanians and Poles also played an important part at different times. Where the North Sea narrows to the English Channel, the Flemish were important members of the Hanseatic League, some belonging to the kingdom of France and others to the Holy Roman Empire.

THE HANSEATIC LEAGUE

However, the merchants of the Middle Ages paid little heed to 'national' frontiers. What mattered to them were the cities and their harbours, mercantile law and counting-houses at which the merchants could meet and make deals. In the towns and cities, people of very different origins lived cheek by jowl. The new cities grew, with their markets acting as a clearing-house for imports and exports. In the early Middle Ages a whole economic community evolved on the shores of the North Sea and the Baltic, which provided the foundation for the development of the Hanseatic League.

Originally the Hansa was a community of merchants, but it survived as a federation of cities into relatively recent times. In the councils of the medieval Hanseatic cities, the merchants set the agenda. The North Sea and the Baltic were linked in a single maritime trading region; commercial ties became closer and required an improved infrastructure.

Continued development was influenced by local rulers or trading co-operatives, who wanted to control trade and expand their own domination of the seas.

Later, the sea power of the Hansa was often talked up, whereas the significance of land routes was given less credit.

Apart from piracy on the high seas, however, it was also the prospect of profit, the search for new lands and a sheer thirst for adventure that drove men to cross the seas in every age: to this day, seafaring holds a fascination for us. We will now follow their medieval course along rivers and coasts and across the seas.

1 RIVERS, COASTS AND SEAS:
NAVIGATION IN THE EARLY MIDDLE AGES

ITINERANT MERCHANTS

In the early Middle Ages shipping routes were crucial to the development of a trade that spanned the North Sea and the Baltic. To transport goods and to seek out remote trading posts, ships were needed. At this time, when merchants travelled, they quite often had to leave their own ships and transfer to other vessels. Two such merchants were Ottar and Wulfstan who, towards the end of the ninth century, reported on their Baltic voyages to the English king, Alfred the Great. Ottar, a Norwegian, had sailed in his own ships along the coasts of the Anglo-Saxon lands, and of Friesland, Norway, Denmark, Sweden and the Slavic countries. Wulfstan, who we believe was English, sailed on a Slav ship from Hedeby (in what is now German Schleswig-Holstein) to the mouth of the Vistula. The same was true of Arab travellers who visited the early trading settlements on the Baltic, as well as of Nordic merchants, who reached Byzantium (now Istanbul) by river routes to the Black Sea. These Swedish Vikings, known to history as the Varangians, later gave the name 'Rus' to the lands along the river Dnieper, now Russia and the Ukraine. It was ships that had made possible the encounters between different merchants. All the peoples who took part in the far-flung commerce around the North Sea and the Baltic built ships. The merchants travelled by a variety of waterways, along rivers and through coastal waters, as well as across the open sea.

River navigation

Rivers linked the hinterland to the sea. Besides local traffic, such as ferries or fishing boats, more substantial quantities of goods were transported for considerable distances along the waterways. To some extent, German rivers like the Rhine, Weser, Elbe and Oder have retained their importance as transport routes. The Vikings also used the rivers for marauding, when they brought their ships up the Rhine, Seine or Thames, to raid cities like London, Cologne, Mainz or Paris.

On the other hand, in Scandinavia, which lacks rivers of any great length, this type of navigation was less important. Nonetheless, in central and northern Sweden, as well as in Finland, rivers and lakes played an important part in the spread of settlement and trade. In summer, light boats could be used, though in winter the rivers and lakes froze over. The Sami, who inhabited what is now Lapland, were among those who possessed boats of skin or bark sewn together over a wooden frame, which could be carried easily. The tradition of lightweight boats goes back a long way. Writing in the late ninth century, the merchant Ottar mentions that the Kven, a people of northern Scandinavia, carried their small light boats overland in what is now northern Sweden, in order to attack the Norwegians on the Atlantic coast.

As far back as Neolithic times, dugout canoes were used by local fisherman. There is even archaeological evidence of clinker-built boats, that is, with hulls constructed from overlapping wooden planks. There have been notable finds of this type in the boat-graves excavated in Valsgärde and Vendel in the Swedish province of Uppland.

Rafts made from tree trunks lashed together were the principal means of ferrying people and goods across rivers, but there were also specialised, flat-bottomed punts, or 'prams'. A pram from around AD 1100 as been found near Egernsund on the Flensburg Fjord between north Germany and Denmark. River prams have also come to light in excavations in Novgorod, and were in use around 1300 for shipping goods across the Öresund, the narrow strait between Denmark and Sweden. Heavy freight was transported downstream on rafts, to be transshipped at seaports. Afterwards, the rafts were dismantled and the logs used for other purposes.

Rivers played an especially large part in the long-distance trade between the Baltic and Byzantium, in which the Varangians, Scandinavian merchants, were prominent. There will be more to say about the role of the Varangians in Chapter 6.

In the wake of the Varangians: a white-water archaeologist

In addition to historical and archaeological evidence, experiments have been carried out to prove how it was possible to travel from the Baltic to the Black Sea along Russian rivers. Between 1983 and 1985 the Swedish archaeologist Erik Nylén completed a boat journey of this kind. His boat, called *Krampacken* (literally 'merchandise bag') was an 8-metre-long copy of a vessel excavated on Gotland, dating from around 1100. Starting from the Baltic, Nylén first took his boat up the river Vistula. The *Krampacken* was then laboriously dragged on wheels over the Dukla pass in the Carpathian mountains. Going down the rivers Tisza and Danube, the expedition finally arrived in the Black Sea. It took a total of 142 days to reach Istanbul (the ancient Byzantium or Constantinople).

Unfortunately, the Soviet authorities had not issued Nylén with a permit to travel along the Pripyet and Dnieper rivers, the 'Route of the

quilz auoient de gene si se par
tirent des pors desfraune et na
tterent vers armozique qui a pre
sent est apxelle bretaigne la pe
tie. S y laisserent poitou a destre
et vndrent tout droit au lieu ou

la riuiere de loire chiet en la met
et entrerent en leaue doulce de
la riuiere en montant vn pou des
poies puis onterent leurs vaisse
aulx z issirent tous dehors et pren
dret terre po'ester esbatz z voir pays

Comment apres ce que brutus et Cormeus auec leurs gene eurent seiour
ne vn iour au bout de loire se mirent en leurs nefs et nagerent contremont
leaue tme quilz trouerent vns lieu conuenable pour eulx aiser ou ilz fiche
rent leurs herbergies et comment ilz desconfirent le roy chauffier dacquitame
Chippire.

[Q]vant il vint a la con
noissance du roy
chuffier de poitiers
que gene estrangies estoient des
cendues en sa terre sans sa licence
Il lui en despleut grandement et

y enuoia tantost vns sien cheual
lier apxelle humbert pour sauoir
quelz gene cestoient et quilz que
royent en son pays. Tant
cheuaucha humbert quil vint pz
des loitis aux troyens si entra de

In both war and peace rivers provided an
important means of transport.
This medieval manuscript shows an
army encampment on the Loire.

Varangians to the Greeks' that we know from medieval chronicles. Had he taken this route, Nylén would only have had to drag his boat 20 km between the two river systems, whereas on the Vistula–Danube route, the vessel had to be transported 490 km over land. Nevertheless, because the waterways they chose were subject to very little regulation, the expedition members were well able to assess the risks and opportunities of such journeys. They covered an average of 17 km per day upstream along the Polish rivers, but 34 km per day downstream along the Tisza and as much as 43 km on the Danube. The overland stretch across the Carpathians was traversed at a rate of 17 km per day. When considering medieval river journeys, the larger difference in speeds upstream and downstream has to be taken into account.

Medieval traders had to negotiate short overland stretches between two rivers, as well as narrow and shallow reaches of the rivers, not to mention the dangerous rapids at the mouth of the Dnieper. Here, a 33-metre drop in height over a distance of 61 km meant coping with nine overfalls with numerous rock barriers, a thundering din and boiling foam and a succession of several waterfalls. Today a hydro-electric dam has totally transformed the estuary of the Dnieper, but then the rapids were frequently described, among others by the Byzantine emperor Constantine VII Porphyrogenitus in AD 944 in the course of his disquisitions on imperial foreign policy.

The rapids and their dangers are brought vividly to life in the names that have come down to us through Greek texts: Essoupi (the Swallower), Baruphoros (Wave-falls), Stroukoun (the Runner), Gelandri (the Shrieker), Oulvorsi (Island-falls) or Leanti (the Laugher). The name of another rapid – Aifur (Ever-loud) – is engraved on a Swedish runic stone at Pilgårds on the island of Gotland. The stone was erected by the four brothers of a Varangian named Rafn, who drowned in the river Dnieper. Other runic stones in Sweden contain a number of indications of the river route to Byzantium. For example, a stone at Sjusta in Uppland province recalls Spialbodi, who met his death in Novgorod, and one in Ed, in the same region, commemorates Rognvald, who led a band of men to Greece.

We also learn from a variety of historical accounts that the rapids became passable when the water level rose as a result of the snow melting in spring. However, it was advisable not to wait too long, since the current became stronger and stronger. Even given quick reactions and a light, highly manoeuvrable type of craft, the journey through the rapids was full of danger. According to Porphyrogenitus, the boats were steered by the natives of Rus, while the crews waded through the shallows beside and ahead of them. The slaves whom they brought with them as merchandise no doubt had to get out of the boats as well. At the fourth stretch of rapids, Aifur, the slaves were led for some 10 km over land. The boats sailed through empty or were carried by land.

Specialised boats were needed for these river and land routes: they had to be suited to the open sea as well as to river journeys, and had to be capable of being pulled. They had to have good sailing qualities and also be easy to row. The hardest thing, in the early Middle Ages, was to transport the boats over land. For this reason alone they could scarcely have been longer than 8 to 10 m (26–33 ft). The Danish marine archaeologist Ole Crumlin-Pederson believes that the boats were dragged with tow-ropes on sled-runners along planks smeared with fat. While the whole crew was busy dragging their boat, they made an easy target for attacks.

The boats they used were described in Greek by Porphyrogenitus as *monoxyla* ('single timbers'), which means that they may have been constructed from a single tree trunk. Boats like this were built upstream from Kiev and floated down the Dnieper after the ice had melted. The Rus bought these dugouts and fitted them with oars and rowlocks, as well as other equipment cannibalised from the previous year's dugouts. Along the whole length of the hull, plank walls from older craft were fitted, in a style that was still seen among the Cossacks in the early modern age. At the same time, these walls were so light that they could easily be carried. These Russian river craft bear a distant resemblance to representations on the carved stones in Gotland.

The Arab writer Ibn Fadlan also mentions specialised ships for transporting goods along rivers, in his description of the burial in AD 922 of a chieftain of the Rus who was laid to rest in his ship. This form of burial reflects a Scandinavian custom. A number of such boat-graves, or more precisely their remains, have been found near Staraya Ladoga, Gnezdovo and around the watershed of the Dnieper river system. Since these burials involved burning the boats, we learn nothing about the appearance of the boats from the finds, except that they were held together with iron rivets.

Coastal navigation

Once the merchants had brought their boats through river estuaries and into the sea, it was essential – unless they decided to tranship their cargoes – to have seaworthy craft. For sea voyages the Norsemen used special ships, the famous crewed long-ships, like those found in the Swedish boat-graves at Vendel and Valsgärde, as well as those in Denmark at Ladby and Hedeby, and the wrecks excavated near Skuldelev. In the accounts of voyages, which King Alfred added to his Anglo-Saxon translation of Orosius' history of the world, we hear from the Norwegian Ottar, who 'lived the farthest north of all the Norsemen'. The descriptions by this merchant and large-scale farmer of his voyages between AD 870 and 890 not only make fascinating reading, but are all the more valuable for having been based on his personal experience. Reproduced here is a slightly abridged version of his account of the voyage to the North Cape and subsequently to Kaupang and Hedeby:

Othere [Ottar] told his lord, King Alfred, that of all the Norsemen, he lived the farthest north. He said that he sailed northwards through the western sea [Norwegian Sea] along the coast, and reports that there the land extends very far northward, but that it is quite desolate apart from a few places here and there where Finns dwell, in order to hunt in winter and catch fish in the summer.

Once, as he recounted, he wanted to find out how far north the land stretched, and where one would come to, north of this deserted region. For this reason he steered due north, keeping close to the land. For three whole days he sailed, leaving the barren land to his right and the open sea to his left. He then found himself as far north as the whale-hunters are accustomed to go. But he sailed further northward, for as far as he could go in three more days. Then the land curved away to the east, or the sea penetrated inland – he did not know which. However, he felt sure that he would pick up a westerly or west-northwesterly wind there. Thereupon he sailed south-east along the coast as far as he could go in three days. There he had to wait again for a wind from the north, because the land turned southward, or the sea made another inroad – he did not know which. He then sailed southwards, keeping close to the shore. He went up a river, because he feared a hostile reception and dared not sail any further, since on the far side of the river the land was densely inhabited. Since leaving his own homeland he had not encountered any cultivation until then, for throughout his voyage the land to his right was peopled only by fishermen, bird-catchers and hunters, and those were all Finns. On his left he had constantly had the open sea.

Now here, the Bjarmer [a Finno-Ugrian tribe] possessed well-farmed terrain, which he was not permitted to set foot on. The land of the Terfinnen [sic] was desolate; only hunters, fishermen and bird-catchers dwelt there. The Bjarmer told him many things, not only about their own country but also about the neighbouring regions.

How much of this was true, he did not know. The Finns and the
Bjarmer appeared to speak roughly the same language. His main
reason for going there was simply to explore the region, though it was
also for the whales and walruses, because the tusks of the latter were
of very good ivory. He brought back some of these tusks to the King...

Ottar reported that the part of the country where he lived was
called Halogaland; no man lived further north than that.
Furthermore, in the south of his country there was a harbour called
'Sciringes heale' (now Kaupang, near the mouth of the Oslo Fjord). He
believed that, if one did not anchor at night and had a fair wind all
day, it would take less than a month to sail there, and the traveller
must sail along the coast all the time. On his starboard side he would
first have Iceland, then the islands which lie between Iceland and our
country (i.e. the Faroes, Shetland and Orkney) then our country (i.e.
England) until he reaches Sciringssal. On his port side, for the entire
voyage lies Norway. South of Sciringssal a great sea [the Baltic] goes
far inland and is so wide that no man can see across it. On the other
side [of the entrance] lies Jutland and further south, Sillende
[Schleswig]. This sea, Ottar says, goes inland for many hundreds of
miles. From Sciringssal, according to his statement, a further five
days' voyage brings the sailor to the harbour that is called Haethum
[Haithabu/Hedeby]. It lies between the lands of the Wends, Saxons
and Angles and is under Danish rule. Sailing thither from Sciringssal
one has on the port side Denmark [south-west Sweden, then under
Danish rule] and on the starboard side a stretch of sea that takes
three days to cross. And for two days before reaching Haethum the
sailor has had Jutland, Sillende and many islands on his starboard
side. In this region lived the Angles before they came to our country
[i.e. England]. And in the same two days he had islands on his port
side, that belong to Denmark...

Thus we learn that Ottar sailed along the coast in search of further profits
to add to his income from farming, fishing and trading. There was a good
market for animal products such as walrus-tusks and skins. The fact that
these journeys to the north were common in his time is clear from the
mention of the whalers' routes. Since this area came within Norway's
economic purview, his description of this as a voyage of exploration is
hardly accurate, since he could make himself understood without an
interpreter to the indigenous Sami (whom he calls Finns). His description
of himself as 'the most northerly Norwegian' should not be taken quite

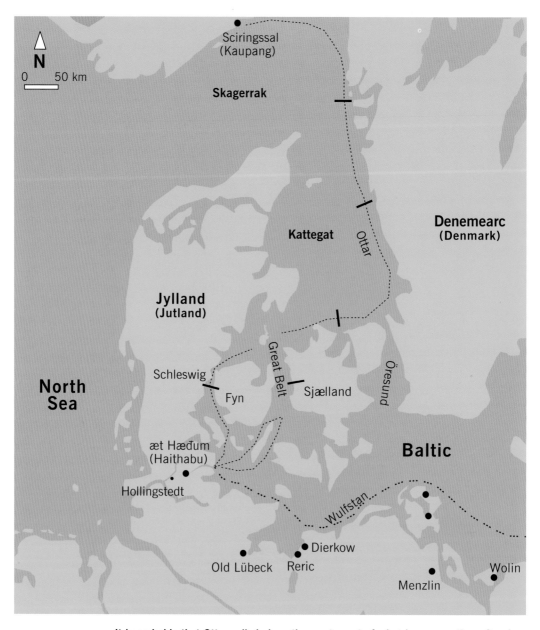

It is probable that Ottar sailed along the west coast of what is now southern Sweden, but was then part of Denmark. He then sailed through the Great Belt channel between the islands of Sjaelland and Fyn, or the Little Belt, between Fyn and Jutland, until he reached Hedeby (Haithabu), a distance of some 400 nautical miles from Kaupang.

literally, even though he may have lived near the limit of Viking settlement at that time. But far to the north of his home there was soon a new settlement of Norwegian Vikings.

However, we can learn from Ottar's account how long the coastal journey took from his home in Hålogaland (in northern Norway) to the North Cape and beyond, as well as to the trading centre of Sciringssal (Kaupang) in southern Norway and to Haedum (Hedeby). The journey down the Norwegian coast to Kaupang, allowing for bad weather and anchoring every night, took about a month. Ottar gives further information about the voyage to Hedeby: this lasted five days and five nights, during which, for the first three days, he had 'Denmark' (by which he means what is now the west coast of Sweden) on his port side and the open sea to starboard. For the last two days the islands belonging to Denmark (Fyn and Sjaelland) lay to port and Jutland, Schleswig and many small islands to starboard.

On this voyage Ottar sailed during the day and anchored at night. This was the only way he could navigate safely through the Danish waters with their many reefs and shallows. With 16 daylight hours for sailing, the ship could make five knots in favourable winds. The nights were spent in the protection of natural harbours. Today there are wrecks off Denmark and Sweden that enable us to locate some of these anchorages. Here there were often local markets on nearby beaches, for instance at the mouth of an inlet. One such was at Lynæs on the Isefjord, on the west side of Sjaelland.

On the south coast of the Baltic, too, there were natural harbours like those at Prerow and Hiddensee (in what is now a national coastal park, north of Stralsund) and at Peenemünde Hook, east of Greifswald. In Jutland we find many natural harbours and beaching places on the coasts. Admittedly, these outlying harbours are scarcely ever mentioned in written sources, but they can be identified through archaeological finds or place names. In Denmark, in the late Middle Ages, these competed with the cities as 'illegal ports' and played a local role in medieval commerce. Sight of land and good places to anchor at night continued to be important in coastal navigation until well into the thirteenth century.

We have evidence of this from the itinerary in the tax register of the Danish king Valdemar; this is the *Jordebog*, a kind of Domesday Book dating from 1230. The sea route described in it, from Blekinge in southern Sweden to Tallinn in Estonia, does not cross the open sea of the Baltic, but keeps close to the Swedish coast, calling at the islands of Öland and Gotland and passing through the skerries to Stockholm. From there it continues to the Åland Islands, in the Gulf of Bothnia, and across to Finland. It then makes the short passage south across the Gulf of Finland to the north coast of Estonia and finally to Tallinn.

In the late Middle Ages, when the compass had become common on merchant ships, seafarers could free themselves from coast-bound navigation. The shipmasters now sailed from landmark to landmark guided by the new navigational instrument. To avoid running aground the lead-line was used, a long cord knotted at intervals, with a lead weight on the end.

The oldest evidence of sailing instructions using a compass is a 'Sea-Book' for the Baltic. Like so much in the evolution of navigation, it came from the Netherlands. However, from the early Middle Ages we also have the account of Wulfstan's voyage, which took him from Hedeby to Truso in the Bay of Danzig (now Gdansk). The sailing ship took seven days and nights, and it is expressly stated that they sailed by night as well. But how was Wulfstan able to do this, when Ottar could not? The answer is simple: the sea area along the southern coast of the Baltic differs from the dangerous shallows among the Norwegian and Swedish skerries, or the fjords and sounds of Denmark. The stretch of the southern Baltic coast that Wulfstan called 'Wend-land', or land of the Slavs, and which he kept on his starboard side on this voyage, is very flat. From the coast out to the open sea, the depth increases steadily and there are no dangerous reefs. Here ships could sail close to the coast by day and night, provided they took soundings and stayed in a depth of 10 to 20 metres. If the water became shallower, they headed out to sea, and when the depth was greater they hugged closer to the land. Although this technique was perfectly good for coastal navigation, it could not be used when the open sea had to be crossed, in order to reach more distant trading posts.

Other medieval sources tell us about the duration of sea voyages. Thus we read in the *Vita Anskarii*, the life of St Ansgar, that a non-stop voyage of 580 nautical miles from Hedeby to Birka, on Lake Mälar near Stockholm, took 20 days, including sailing at night. In the eleventh century, Adam of Bremen tells us that the 1,100 nautical mile journey from Denmark to Novgorod took 30 days without stopping. These two examples are really only an indication of what was theoretically possible in the best ships. The average speed on long-distance voyages was around 30 nautical miles per day or 60 nautical miles (110 km) when sailing by night and day.

High-seas navigation

In the early Middle Ages shipping in northern Europe was not, however, restricted to rivers and coastal journeys; voyages were undertaken across the Baltic and North Sea, and from the ninth or tenth centuries even across the North Atlantic. Those daring seamen were thus deep-water sailors. When, at the end of the tenth century, Ottar sailed to England, his course took him from the west coast of Norway to the Shetland Islands and Scotland, then southward down the east coast of England. This route was well known in the early Middle Ages and needed no special acclaim. It was a convenient way to reach the Humber and Thames estuaries, the gateways to northern and southern England respectively. Some time before AD 1000, Erik the Red set out from Iceland and sailed as far as Greenland. Later voyages took him to Newfoundland. We will return to this in Chapter 7.

2 EXPERIENCE AND INNOVATION:
SHIPBUILDING IN THE MIDDLE AGES

THE EVOLUTION OF SHIPBUILDING

After the collapse of the Roman Empire and the shadowy period of the *Völkerwanderung*, or westward migration in Europe, trade experienced a revival in the early Middle Ages. The Rhine had never quite lost its role as an important transport route to England. With the expansion of the Frankish empire, a new power had arisen in central Europe. Even though the Franks were able to gain a foothold in the Rhine/Meuse/Scheldt delta, they remained nevertheless a continental rather than a maritime power. The estuaries in the marshland of the Netherlands were controlled by the Friesians, the northern Baltic by Danish and Swedish Vikings and its southern coast by Slavic tribes.

The ships that plied the North Sea and the Baltic were chiefly Scandinavian and Friesian, but some Slav vessels were among them. The Scandinavian regions imported handmade products and luxury goods from central Europe. In addition to trade and commerce, the Vikings also carried out swift pillaging raids. Their ships were particularly suited to the latter, since they could come in from the open sea, sail up the rivers and, where there were no harbours, could run up on shelving beaches. This made surprise attacks possible, as well as simple trading transactions. The Vikings possessed long, narrow and fast warships and beamier trading ships that could carry more cargo. In this way, the foundations for differentiated forms of ship construction were already laid in the early Middle Ages in northern Europe.

With the development of maritime cities in the High Middle Ages, the demands on cargo capacity in ships became ever greater. But now the new seagoing ships had a deeper draught. They therefore had to unload their cargoes at seaports lying at the tidal limit and were no longer able to sail so far inland up the rivers. The enlarged freight capacity had in turn to be matched by an increased flow of goods, otherwise the ships would not have paid their way. The growing cities provided the markets that were needed. From the late Middle Ages onward, new sea routes were added to the traditional routes plied for centuries by the Friesians, Saxons, English and Scandinavians.

The ships in northern Europe had thus developed to meet the demands of trade. The decisive factor was the ability to exploit the wind with sail. Since sail had been familiar in the Mediterranean for several millennia BC, one might have expected this innovation to be taken up rapidly in the north. However, that did not happen. Around the birth of Christ the commercial cities of the Mediterranean were served by merchant ships with a large mainsail and a small foresail (*artemon* in Greek). The Celts had used sail along the coast of Normandy since 100 BC. The Germanic races adopted the Celtic word *sagulum*, whence *segel* in modern German and Swedish, and 'sail' in English. However, those sails were of leather, unlike the Roman sails made from linen (*velum*), whence *vela* in Italian and Spanish and *voile* in French.

It was the sailing ship that first made it possible to cover large distances. Neither the skin-covered canoes with planks sewn together, which had been used in the north since the Bronze Age, nor the later oared boats, were able to make more than short trips. However, initially the freedom provided by sail had its limits, and the first sailing vessels remained fair-weather craft. From the long, narrow boats of the Iron Age and the Viking period, ship design evolved to the medieval 'cog' and finally to the carrack and the caravel. The first ships had a single mast and a rectangular sail, then further masts were added. The hull construction also evolved from clinker-building, with overlapping planks nailed together, to the carvel technique, in which the edges of the planks are planed and fitted flush, giving the ship a smooth outer skin. The following is an outline of the development of shipbuilding in the north, up to the late Middle Ages, chiefly based on archaeological finds and a few contemporary depictions.

THE DAWN OF SHIPBUILDING

The earliest ventures on to the water in northern Europe were made in dugouts and canoes such as the Hjortspring boat. Hjortspring, on the Danish island of Als at the entrance to the Flensburg Fjord, is where sacrifices to the gods had been buried in the boggy land. The remains were found of what had once been a 19-m long craft from the period around 350 BC, which had room for a crew of 22. This boat was suitable for lake and river work, and could also cover fairly short distances along the coast. Its planks were bound with twine to each other and to the cross-ribs.

It was only with the construction of larger wooden ships, which could be rowed and sailed, that it became possible to make longer voyages along rivers and across the sea. It was no longer the muscle power of the men wielding paddles or oars that determined a vessel's range, but the wind. However, voyages were restricted both by the limited knowledge of navigation and by the seaworthiness of the boats. The seamen also had to master a new technique of steering. When sailing with the wind abeam, the leeway, or sideways drift, had to be kept as small as possible, in order to manoeuvre using the changing direction and strength of the winds.

As already mentioned, the Celts used sailing craft on the north coast of France. Writing in AD 69, the Roman historian Tacitus observes that the Germanic tribes who took part in the uprising of the Batavii launched a fleet operation, with warships captured from the Romans and with a large number of local vessels, crewed by 30 to 40 men and fitted with brightly painted leather sails. His contemporary, Pliny the Elder, describes how the tribes of northern Gaul, among whom leather sails were common in pre-Roman times, later wove linen sails and how the 'enemies of the empire beyond the Rhine' (i.e. the Germanic peoples) made use of this innovation.

Very few ships have survived from the period from the end of the Roman empire to the beginning of the early Middle Ages. All the more significant, then, were the discoveries made between 1859 and 1863 in a bog near Nydam on the Flensburg Fjord. As well as numerous weapons, the archaeologist Claus Engelhard found the remains of at least three large vessels. Like the weapons, these had been offered as sacrifices. On 18 August 1863 Engelhard came upon his most famous find, the 23.5-m-long oak-built vessel, now known as the 'Nydam Ship', which can be seen today in the Landesmuseum [provincial museum] in Schleswig, north Germany.

An examination of the tree-rings in the timbers (dendrochronology) dates the vessel to around AD 320. The large, crewed ship, was clinker-built, with overlapping planks joined with iron rivets. All along the ship, at the top of the ribs to which the planks were fastened were carved heads of men. The ship also had a side-rudder and rowlocks carved from forked branches. While travelling at sea, such ships would navigate from landmark to landmark along the coast. Whether, at this time there were Nordic ships with sails, we do not know, since a ship of the Nydam type would have needed only a few small modifications to take a mast and sail.

In 1945, during the canalisation of the Kongeå river in southern Denmark, a number of well-preserved ship's planks were found. It is probable that this ship had played a part in the commerce between Denmark and the southern and more northerly coasts of the North Sea. The ship still displays elements that could be interpreted as derivative from the Nydam type; however, in this vessel we see for the first time evidence of the strong fixing of ribs to the outer skin of the hull. The Gredstedbro Ship, as it is called, is probably the oldest example of a sailing vessel that sailed off the coast of Ribe, south of modern Esbjerg.

The Byzantine historian Procopius gives the following account of ships of the Angles in England around the year AD 560: 'These barbarians use no sail to propel themselves, only oars.' Not even the ship belonging to the Anglo-Saxon king Redwald, at the beginning of the seventh century AD, boasted a mast, if we are to judge from the remains found at the Sutton Hoo burial in Suffolk. On the other hand, it was wind that drove Beowulf's ship as mentioned in the Introduction.

THE VIKING AGE

Even today, the Viking period prompts us to see ships as the symbol of an entire epoch. In the early days of the Viking age, if not before, we see the development of beamy cargo ships and more slender warships, both with sails. Equipped with these, the Scandinavians were able to thrust southwards on trading and marauding expeditions. It was with the attack on Lindisfarne, off the Northumbrian coast, in 793 that the Norsemen first attracted attention and soon earned the name 'Viking'. Later the Norsemen settled in northern France, which became known as Normandy and its inhabitants Normans. Finally, in 1066, William of Normandy invaded England. The Viking age was over, but for some time afterwards ships built in the Nordic or Viking tradition were still seen on the seas.

Viking boat construction

The first idea we obtained of the wide variety of Viking-age vessels came about in 1957, in the Danish town of Skuldelev, where a barrier made of ships' hulls was discovered on the bottom of the Roskilde Fjord. Here lay long, narrow warships, and broad-beamed freighters, as well as smaller fishing boats and ferries dating from the period 1030–1050. What all Viking ships have in common are the stem- and stern-posts curving up to an equal height, hewn from a single piece of timber and fixed to the keel. These gave the ships an elegant appearance. The hull was clinker-built, fixed with iron nails to the keel, to the stem and sternposts and to each other. The basic elements of clinker construction, with overlapping planks, date back to before the middle of the first millennium, in the areas along the Baltic coasts settled by northern Germanic tribes. The most famous find – as already mentioned – comprised the three large fourth-century boats from the bog at Nydam, of which only one has been preserved.

Only after the clinkered planks had formed the outer skin of the craft was the sub-frame of equidistant ribs fitted. These were not fixed to the keel, a fact that gave the ship greater elasticity. The cross-beams between the ribs served as supports for the oarsmen's benches (thwarts) or for the deck. In the centre of the ship the mast was located, held firmly in a mast-shoe, a lengthwise beam fixed to the keel. In older ships, the mast was held at deck height by a massive cross-beam. This design requires a particularly strong keel, which was therefore usually made from a single huge beam.

The trading ships or merchantmen, such as Ship 3 found at Skuldelev, differed from the long, narrow fighting ships, by having a deeper and broader hull space. The decking at the bow and stern accommodated the lookout and the steersman respectively. The oars of Viking ships were located towards the stern. There was little protection for the oarsmen, who sat along the sides of the ship. The cargo was probably covered with skins. On the single mast hung a wide sail, which gave good headway with winds abaft the beam.

To date we only know of a few places where Viking vessels were built or repaired. These include Wolin, near Szczecin in Poland, Paviken on Gotland and Hedeby.

Ships as religious symbols

The Vikings brought shipbuilding in northern Europe to a hitherto unseen peak of perfection. Ships were far more than mere means of transport. The Norse sagas, and the images the Norsemen carved on stone, emphasise the importance of ships in mythology, just as do the Viking-age graves marked with boat-shaped lines of stones, such as those in the burial-fields in Lindholm Høje on the Limfjord in northern Jutland, and the burials in boats beneath mounds. The ship provided the last crossing to Valhalla, into the world of the gods. No wonder, then, that ships became symbols of exceptionally high status.

Boats or ships with burial chambers built on to them have been found at several sites in Norway, dating from the eighth to the tenth centuries. This form of grave apparently harks back to an older tradition. This is shown by the ship-grave at Sutton Hoo in Suffolk, dating from the early seventh century, and the carved stones on Gotland from the fifth and sixth centuries. The custom of burying the dead in boats is not only traceable over a fairly long period, from the Dark Age migrations up to the Viking age, but is typical of seafaring races in northern Europe. Both men and women were interred with a variety of precious grave-goods.

It was in Oseberg, in south-western Norway, that a royal ship from the period around AD 820 was first excavated. To judge from its construction, the vessel was mainly intended for coastal and inland waters, but may have served no purpose other than to carry a king on his final journey. From another Norwegian grave, that of Gokstad, came a Viking ship that is an unrivalled masterpiece of marine construction. This ship, which tree-ring

The Nydam Ship dates from around AD 320. It was found in a marsh on the Danish island of Als, near the modern border with Germany.

On pictorial stones found in Gotland we see both oared vessels and sailing ships. The early ships from the sixth and seventh centuries are usually depicted without sails, while those from the eighth to twelfth centuries have sails. Seven stones depict large vessels with up to ten oarsmen and two helmsmen. In the middle of the ship a tent was erected for protection. In the oldest images the sails are depicted schematically as small rectangles. The picture-stones of latest date show the famous Viking ships with square sails and rigging.

dating puts at between AD 895 and 900, was one of the vessels in which the Norsemen crossed the seas. Both well-preserved ships can be seen today in the Bygdøy Museum in Oslo. Although the Gokstad Ship was less richly ornamented than that of Oseberg, its design is superb and was in an excellent state of preservation when it was discovered. Its seaworthiness was proved shortly afterwards, when, in 1880, a replica crossed the North Atlantic from Norway to the United States at speeds of up to 11 knots.

In addition to the ships discovered along the Oslo Fjord and in Skuldelev, there were numerous similar finds in the Baltic region. In the area around Lake Mälar, west of Stockholm, were found the boat-graves of Vendel and Valsgärde mentioned earlier. The principal finds here were boats of 7 m to 10 m in length; these were crewed by three to seven pairs of oarsmen and were used in fjords and other inland and coastal waters. Even shorter boats of less than 5m were used on rivers or as tenders to larger craft.

The most important of the larger grave-ships was that found at Ladby on the Danish island of Fyn. Here a Viking long-ship was discovered under a burial-mound. Excavation of the site, on a low hill 100 m south of the Kerteminde Fjord, revealed bodies buried intact as well as cremated, though with almost no grave-goods. Some 3 km further to the east, the fjord runs into the Great Belt channel, and the ship probably came up the narrow fjord to reach its final resting place. Today the mound has been covered over again, but the visitor can climb down a stairway to view the impressive remains inside.

Outside the semicircular rampart, which enclosed the settlement of Hedeby, a highly placed personage was buried in a boat-tomb that was excavated in 1908. Unlike the other Viking-age ship-burials, the grave consists of a large underground chamber beneath the ship. In the western half of the tomb a corpse was found, with valuable grave-goods: costly weapons, saddles and stirrups, horses, personal jewellery and tableware, indicating the high standing of the deceased. There was a glass beaker that came from Charlemagne's empire. The sword buried with the man was probably made in the north from a Carolingian design. Separated from this by a wall of tree trunks was a less richly appointed burial in the eastern part of the chamber. The high-ranking person was probably followed to his death by two companions. To the east of the wooden chamber lay three horse skeletons, pointing east–west. In contrast to similar excavated grave-ships, no large mound was thrown up over the boat-tomb; instead the ship was filled with sand and stones and only surrounded by a low mound. The excavation found no remains of the ship itself, other than the iron rivets.

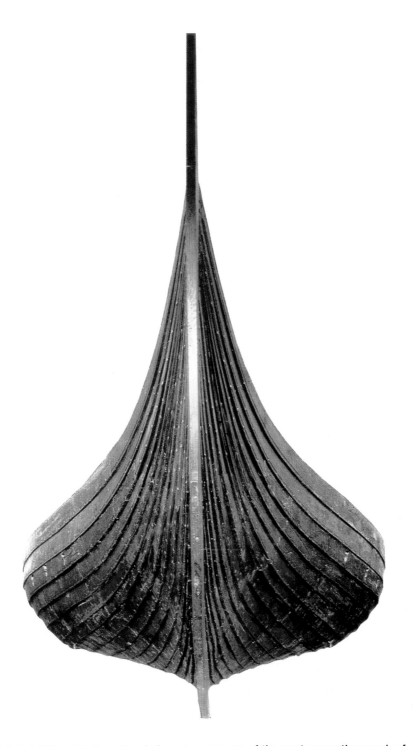

The Gokstad Viking ship from the ninth century was one of the most seaworthy vessels of its day. The picture clearly shows the 'clinker' construction of overlapping planks.

The reconstructed dimensions of the Hedeby Ship (length 17–20 m, and beam 2.7–3.5 m) were similar to those of the ship found at Ladby.

The boat-tomb was constructed at a time when weapons, glass drinking-vessels, and belt buckles of Carolingian design were already in common use. At the same time, however, forms of riding equipment appeared, which have been found in the row-graves of the south-west Baltic region and in central Sweden, dating from the first half of the tenth century. One can only surmise that the man buried in the Hedeby boat-tomb, with two of his loyal followers, was the conqueror of Hedeby, King Olaf of Sweden. According to the *Annals of Lund* (the old university town near Malmö), the grave must have been prepared in 906, the year of Olaf's death. However, the lack of more reliable historical sources makes it impossible to connect the tomb with the Swedish ruler. At any event, the grave-goods clearly illustrate the cultural exchange between Scandinavia and the Frankish empire, a process in which seafaring played a crucial role.

In 1903 this magnificently decorated royal burial-ship was excavated at Oseberg on the Oslo Fjord.

The Oseberg and Gokstad ships have a length-to-beam ratio of 4.1:1, and 4.7:1 respectively, which makes them relatively broad. The equivalent ratios of the Sutton Hoo, Ladby and Hedeby finds range from 5.7:1 to 6.4:1, which puts them in the narrow-beam category. These were large, seaworthy craft, rowed by crews of 30 to 40 men. They had a mast that could be dismantled, giving them good manoeuvrability and an advantage as fighting ships.

Wrecks from the Viking period

As well as the ships that served as graves, numerous wrecks from the Viking period have been found in the Baltic. Many of the ships never reached their destination; they either sank or ran aground. In storms, ships could be lost in the open sea, but just as often near the coast, especially in narrow channels and sounds like Denmark's Great and Little Belts, where there are dangerous currents. Time and again, maps of the various shipwrecks show how most vessels foundered in the same places near the coast, in the Kattegat and the Skagerrak, in the sounds and Belts. A number of these wrecks can, by their location, reveal hitherto unknown places where ships beached for trading purposes in the early Middle Ages. However, it is less easy to determine the exact origin of the ships.

BOATBUILDING AMONG THE SLAVS

Scandinavian boatbuilding also influenced the ships of the Slav inhabitants of the southern Baltic coast, who chiefly adopted the clinker building technique. Unlike the Scandinavians, the Slavic tribes made no use of iron, and preferred wooden dowels to rivets. However, both building traditions were often combined, as shown by finds in southern Scandinavia and the southern Baltic coast.

A further feature typical of Slavic boatbuilding was caulking with moss or wool and sealing with tar. The boats usually had flat bottoms. Near Ralswiek on the north German island of Rügen, the remains of three ships lying side by side came to light during archaeological excavations between 1966 and 1968. These boats must have plied the Baltic in the ninth or tenth centuries and were then pulled out of the water and broken up ashore. We do not know whether their owners were among the pirates who later, in the eleventh and twelfth centuries, were to terrorise the western Baltic. During a storm the water rose abnormally high, washed over the beached boats and covered them with sand. Nevertheless, archaeologists were able to recognise the boats by their technical features. For example, the oak planks were assembled in clinker fashion, like the Viking ships; the lengthways planks were fastened with iron rivets, and the overlapping planks were sealed, or caulked, as seamen say, with tar or pitch. The planks were fixed to the cross-ribs with wooden dowels, and iron nails were used for other fixings. One of the boats was 14 m long and had a beam of 3.4 m; the second was 9.5 m long and 2.5 m wide. These craft could sail well, and if there was no wind, were powered by eight to ten oarsmen. The cargo capacity would have been something between one and two tonnes.

At a site on the north side of the Danish island of Falster, boats in the Slavic tradition were built and repaired in the late eleventh century. The name of the place, Sknekkeberg, is an echo of the Danish word *sknekk*, a component in the construction of war-ships (*sknekkjas*) in the Viking age and the Middle Ages. In the archaeological excavations 1,700 parts of several ships were recovered, whose planks were held together with wooden dowels.

FROM THE VIKING SHIP TO THE COG

With the growth of trade the need arose for larger ships with greater cargo capacity. Although the Baltic is an almost landlocked sea, the ships that plied it were as large as those in the North Sea and Atlantic: the wrecks of large warships and merchant ships have been found both in Hedeby and Skuldelev. These probably saw service both in the North Sea and the Baltic. Historical evidence points to long voyages being made by large merchant ships in the twelfth century. So, in the *Miracle of St Thomas of Canterbury* from around 1175, a large vessel is described, which was built for the king of Denmark by a rich burgher of Schleswig. But just as with the *Vasa*, the Swedish royal vessel that sank in Stockholm harbour in the seventeenth century, immediately after its launch, here too ambition overreached reality. The Danish ship was so heavy that despite every effort, using rollers and tow ropes, it could not be launched. There was great disappointment, as we read:

> *Everyone could see that the ship had to be broken up. However, in order that the despondent ship-owner should not see his efforts and financial outlay go to waste, he decided to obtain the blessing of the new martyr, Thomas of Canterbury. He addressed the saintly effigy with the words: bring the said vessel into deep water, O Martyr, and I promise you from each of its trading voyages one hundred pounds of wax. With bare hands and with far less applied force than before, they set the ship in motion and, sliding on something smooth, it then plunged with ease into the waves. And the undertaking to which the merchant had given his solemn vow exists to our own day.* (Thomas de Froidmont: The Life of Saint Thomas Becket, Archbishop of Canterbury)

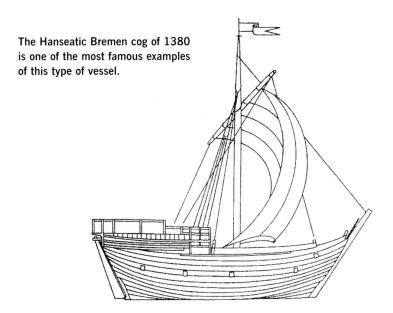

The Hanseatic Bremen cog of 1380 is one of the most famous examples of this type of vessel.

Yet despite this misfortune, in the twelfth century the size of warships and merchant ships grew compared to ships of the Viking age. True, shipbuilding remained a matter of personal experience, yet there was no clinging to ancient tradition; innovations were made, which carried shipbuilding forward, as we shall see.

THE COG

In the High Middle Ages innovation took the form of new types of ship and improvements in construction techniques. At the start of these developments stands the cog, which typically had a flat bottom and steeply angled stem- and sternposts. Its central mast carried a square-rigged sail.

Early forms of cog

The prototype of a cog had developed over the centuries from a simple dugout with a flat bottom, steep side-walls and tapering, stem-like ends, of the type used in the Friesian sea marshes around AD 800. In the course of time, the dugout was split and the two halves were pushed apart so that floor-planks could be fitted in. On the upper edges of the half-dugouts, additional planks were added, clinker-fashion and fixed with iron staples. To make the early cogs watertight, moss was used. With their flat-bottomed hulls, the cogs were ideal for navigating among the shallow, tidal reedbeds. When coming ashore, the cogs were brought in at high tide and left safely high and dry to be unloaded. Sometimes, horse-drawn carts came right up to the craft to make loading and unloading easier. When the rising tide came up beneath the upward curve of the stern it gave the cog enough lift to enable it float off and sail away.

The cog in pictures and documents

In the ninth century cog-shaped ships appear for the first time on coins struck in Hedeby. Since there was a Friesian community there, it is probable that they began building their early cogs in Danish Hedeby. The Friesians also had a trading colony in the Swedish town of Birka, on Lake Mälar, where they built simple cogs from the tenth century onwards. When Birka died out around AD 1000, a Friesian trading guild grew up in Sigtuna, the town that replaced it. The earliest written references to cogs are found in documents from Utrecht from the ninth and tenth centuries. Here the term *cogsult* is used, meaning the obligation to fit out a cog for service in war. The name *Cokingi* was given to the Friesians, presumably referring to the boats they sailed. In the *Summarium Heinrici*, a medieval reference work for scholars, we read of short-hulled ships called *kogcho*. From 1200 onwards, evidence in historical and literary texts becomes more frequent.

The official seals of Hanseatic cities from the thirteenth and fourteenth centuries show how widespread the seagoing cogs were in the Middle Ages: their home ports stretched from the North Sea to the Baltic.

The Hanseatic cog

With the founding of the Hanseatic League and the rise in commerce, by the end of the twelfth century existing types of ship were no longer adequate. While the basic Friesian cog style was retained, the ships were built longer and with higher freeboard. By rounding the originally angular joins between the sides and the bottom, they were made more seaworthy. The large Hanseatic cogs could no longer be steered with the Friesian side-rudder, so that by 1200 all cogs were fitted with a rudder at the stern. Unlike the Viking ships, the cogs could not be run up on gently sloping beaches; because of its squared-off stem-post, the cog would have become stuck in the sand or mud. When used in the sea marshes, the cog would be brought as close to shore as possible, then left while the tide receded and unloaded when high and dry. This meant that in the sea marshes of the Friesian coast, at least, the early cogs needed no harbours.

Beyond the marshes and other coasts with a large

tidal range, conditions were different. Here the cogs could only anchor in deep water and had to be unloaded with lighters. Since this was awkward and time-consuming, the need for wharfs and harbour facilities became ever more pressing. True, manoeuvring alongside these quays was far less easy than simply running ashore as the Vikings did. If the shipmaster did not handle the sails correctly the ship could easily ram the quayside and spring a leak. From late medieval pictorial sources, we know that the only aids used were long poles. To make mooring easier, many hands were needed. Once the vessel was tied up, gangplanks were lowered for people and freight. From the Hanseatic period onward there were also cranes, with which heavy goods could be raised from the hold, using the lever principle.

However, it was not just peaceful trading but mercantile wars that drove technical innovation. In the late thirteenth century, when the Hansa was at war with Norway, the League followed the English example and fitted its large cogs with castle-like fighting-towers at the bow and stern, in order to give the crossbowmen the highest possible firing position. Since these fighting platforms were also intended to offer protection from the weather,

A replica of a Viking dragon-ship is silhouetted against the midnight sun.

they were given walls – the cabin was born! A seal of Stralsund, dating from 1329, shows for the first time one of these living areas in the aftercastle. As early as 1380 the Bremen cog had various rooms in its aftercastle, with bunks along the outer walls and even the luxury of its own lavatory. From the thirteenth century onwards, there were fireplaces on board, so that the preparation of hot meals greatly improved the quality of shipboard life. In the remains of cogs dating from the late thirteenth century, the ovens consisted of wooden boxes lined with sand or clay and with a flat stone lid, on top of which a fire could be kept alight for long periods, provided the ship did not roll too much. In a heavy sea the embers had to be put out, since, if they had slid off the oven, the ship could have caught fire.

Remains and reconstructions of cogs

The most advanced development of the cog design was the Hanseatic Bremen cog. There was a sensation when on 8 October 1962 a well-preserved wreck was discovered in the silt of the river Weser. A ten-year archaeological project revealed that the cog was not quite finished when, in 1380, it broke loose from the slipway. Since it had no ballast on board it quickly capsized. The ship had shattered into some 2,000 separate pieces and had to be carefully reassembled. With the rebuilding and conservation measures completed, the vessel can be seen today in the German Shipping Museum (Deutsche Schiffahrtsmuseum) in Bremerhaven. Its length is 23.27 m and the maximum beam is 7.62 m. Its height amidships was 4.26 m, making it twice as high as the cargo ships of the Vikings. The hull walls were made up of 12 planks on each side. A particular feature is the transition from the carvel technique (planks laid edge to edge) on the bottom of the hull, to clinker building for the sides. The shipwrights constructed the outer shell of the ship first, and only then were the cross-ribs of naturally curved wood inserted. A massive cross-beam supported the deck structure. In the stern was a low aftercastle with an enclosed cabin. Only the senior officers were accommodated here; the rest of the crew had to sleep in the open as before. The rudder, which has not survived, was fitted on the sternpost. The oak trees used in the construction were felled in a forest in Hessen and floated downstream on the Weser. The 22-metre-tall mast carried a sail with a sail-area of some 210 sq. metres. The ship weighed about 55 tonnes and could carry a cargo of some 90 tonnes. The capacity of the hold was nearly 160 cu. metres. Unladen, the ship had a draft of only 1.25 m, which increased to 2.25 m when fully laden.

After seeing the long, elegant Viking ships, one tends not to attribute great sailing qualities to the tubby and ponderous-looking cogs. But experiments have shown the contrary. A replica cog, using the hull dimensions and sail area deduced from archaeology, has demonstrated astonishing sailing and handling qualities. The Bremen cog could sail at 60 degrees to the wind – surprisingly high for a medieval vessel – and in a fresh wind could theoretically reach 10 knots. Nevertheless, the seamen had to guard against running on to a lee shore; onshore winds would drive the ships into a shallow water and then aground. The number of wrecked cogs on exposed coasts bears witness to this danger.

Important though the Bremen cog is in the history of shipbuilding, it still only gives us a partial view of late medieval seafaring. By now the number of cogs found has greatly increased. To judge from the totality of the finds, the Bremen cog seems to have been among the larger vessels of that period. Not all the vessels discovered had the mast amidships; in some it was stepped further forward, and the ships differed in other details. In the polders of the Ijsselmeer, Holland's inland sea, nearly two dozen wrecks have now been found, along with others in Danish and Swedish waters. The cogs recovered had very different dimensions. The largest cog discovered so far, in the Netherlands, was about 17 m long, with a beam of about 3.5 m.

A replica of the Bremen cog from the Hanseatic period demonstrates its sailing qualities on the Kiel Fjord.

A few years ago parts of a large medieval cog were revealed on the island of Poel off the Baltic coast of Germany, when a storm washed away some of the sand. Aerial photography and help from local fishermen then led to the discovery of the wreck. Since the preservation of the wreck was at risk, it was excavated by archaeologists in the winter of 1999–2000. The wreck's very good state of preservation made a full reconstruction possible. In 2000, archaeologists, naval architects and builders of wooden boats built a replica in the town harbour of Wismar. The *Poeler Kogge* (*Cog of Poel*) made her maiden voyage in 2004.

Another cog can be seen in the Museum of Marine Archaeology in Sassnitz, on the island of Rügen, off the Baltic coast of Germany. On its last voyage the vessel, built around 1330, was carrying a valuable cargo of stone slabs from the Swedish island of Öland, probably bound for Stralsund. There they were perhaps intended for laying as a floor in a church or in aristocratic houses. The cog never reached port because it foundered and sank off the Gellen, a narrow channel between the islands of Rügen and Hiddensee. While some of the cog's cargo and fittings can be seen in the museum in Sassnitz, the limestone slabs have ended up in the lobby of the provincial government building in Schwerin. The 'Gellen Cog' is very interesting from a technical point of view since its builders were attempting to combine the hallowed Baltic manner of clinker building with the carvel technique from the Mediterranean. The result was an unusually thick double skin on the hull, of a kind never before seen in a cog.

However, the reasons for the success of the cog lay not only in its greater cargo capacity – for a 'big ship' found in Bergen and built in the Scandinavian clinker style was competitive both technically and in its cargo capacity – but in the political and economic circumstances of the Hanseatic period. By the fifteenth century the age of the cog was over.

THE CARRACK

Towards the end of the Middle Ages the cog made way for the carrack. This type of ship could also look back on a long tradition As early as 795 Charlemagne had silver *denarii* minted with the image of a carrack in his northern ports – Quentovic near Etaples in northern France and in the (originally) Frieisian port of Dorestad, near modern Utrecht. Later monarchs such as Ludwig the Pious (814–40) followed his example. The coins show an undecked, banana-shaped ship with a mast, which bore a cross as a sign of peaceable trading activity. At the waterside markets, where the ships berthed, a corresponding market cross was set up, indicating peaceful and lawful trading.

Early forms of carrack

As early as AD 800 the carrack was the most important type of ship carrying cargo between England and the Continent, and it remained common until the fourteenth century, in areas west of today's Ijsselmeer. The carrack's reinforced bottom could withstand grounding and the vessel could be left high and dry without difficulty. With its rounded bow and relatively shallow draught, it could easily be run up on any gently shelving, sandy beach. The carrack's shallow draft made it an ideal vessel for trading along the North Sea coast in the early Middle Ages, and merchants established themselves in the numerous waterside markets that were growing up in places like Dorestad, near modern Utrecht on the lower Rhine, Emden at the mouth of the Ems, and Ribe on the west coast of Jutland. Admittedly, the carrack's sailing qualities were – to put it bluntly – appalling. In any side-wind it drifted hopelessly to leeward. For this reason the mast was stepped very far forward; even then it could only sail with the wind aft. It was often necessary to wait a long time in harbour for a favourable wind.

Evolution of the carrack to a large vessel

In the late Middle Ages the small, flat-bottomed craft evolved into a large ship. From damage claims and customs registers we learn of their cargo capacity and performance. As a rule the carrack could carry 200 to 300 tonnes of cargo, such as salt in barrels, and was manned by a crew of 35 to 40 men. Carracks could not carry more cargo than cogs of the same size, but the late medieval carrack may have been more robust and better suited to long voyages, though this is no more than speculation.

English sources tell us that the carrack (then also known as a 'hulk', from the German *Holk*) frequently plied the southern North Sea and the Channel in the eleventh and twelfth centuries, and from the mid-fourteenth century the ship appears quite frequently in Hanseatic sources. The speed with which the carrack established itself is shown by two pieces of historical evidence: around 1380 the Tallinn Customs Book mentions cogs and carracks in overseas commerce, along with unspecified ships. Only twenty years later the grand fleet of the Teutonic Knights consists almost exclusively of carracks. These vessels sailed mainly on the western route to Flanders and western France. The port of Lübeck, which had far fewer trading contacts with the Flemish cities than Danzig did, clung longer to the cog.

The Danzig Seal of 1400 no longer features a cog, only a carrack. In contrast to the cog, the carrack not only had living accommodation in the aftercastle, but also under the elevated forecastle. (To this day, the space in the forward end of a ship is called the fo'c'sle, pronounced 'foke-sul'.) Near

This Baltic chart from 1526, the *Caerte van de Oosterscher Zee* by the Dutchman Jan van Hoirne, shows a small coastal craft (far right) and a Dutch *hulck* or carrack. The *hulck* is drawn from the starboard quarter, astern. We see the wind blowing with full force into the mainsail and foresail. Above the yard-arm is the crow's-nest, and above that a small topsail can be seen. The mizzen-mast in the stern is not properly drawn but carries a lateen, or fore-and-aft, sail. In the fifteenth century large ships of this kind were often to be seen in the North Sea and the Baltic.

the top of the mast there was a further fighting position, called the 'crow's-nest', which later came to be used as a look-out platform. A ship of this kind is described in the Danzig Chronicle of 1465 as a 'grand old carrack'.

With permanent accommodation for the crew, a keel, a more streamlined hull below the waterline and as many as three masts, the carrack represented a considerable advance on the cog. However, like the cog, it still did not have a watertight deck. The substructure of the deck rested on large cross-beams, whose covered ends jutted out beyond the hull of the ship. Hence all the spray or solid water that landed on the deck found its way downward and collected there. The stability of the high-sided ship was not affected provided there was not too much water, and it could be baled out again. However, for the cargoes it was disastrous, since they got soaked. Therefore any goods that had to stay dry were packed in barrels. All these high-sided vessels had, of course, evolved from open boats and hence remained extremely wet.

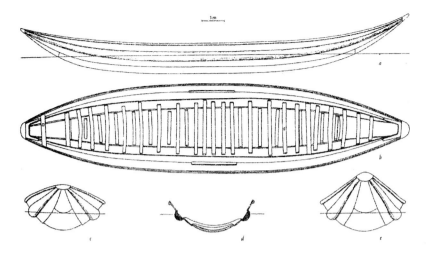

This early *hulck* was excavated in Utrecht, Netherlands, in 1930. It has the typical banana-shaped hull.

The archaeology of carracks

In addition to written and illustrative sources, we have an impression of these ships from archaeology. The dating of an 18.4 m-long carrack excavated in Utrecht in 1930 is disputed, but it belongs to a type that was built between 800 and some time in the twelfth century. Its mast was stepped about one-third of the way along the hull. Its rounded bottom was a single baulk 14.3 m long, reinforced by numerous bottom-planks. The stem- and sternposts were also single timbers fixed to the keel. These gave the ship a pronounced sheer, that is to say a downward and upward sweep in the deck-line, since the fore and aft section were much high than the middle. The sheer prevented waves from breaking over the bow or stern and meant that the ship could be sailed on the open sea. Fixed to the rounded bottom timber were three planks fitted clinker fashion, each fastened with wooden dowels to the one below.

While this vessel represented an early form of carrack, Dutch marine archaeologists later brought to light a larger ship in Flevoland. The planks from the bottom of this carrack had clearly been sawn – the first time this had been found. However, the side-planks had been split from wood. This shows that the boatbuilders of the time were mentally freeing themselves from the idea of hewing the bottom from a single tree-trunk, since in the early carracks the bottom-planks had also been hewn. Nor were the clinker-laid planks of this ship fastened with wooden dowels, but with iron rivets. The Flevoland carrack, dating from the fifteenth century, certainly had two masts, possibly three, for the growing size of the ship demanded a larger sail-area to drive it forward. This in turn could only be achieved with several masts, as had been customary in the Mediterranean since the fifteenth century. In the long term, handling the sails required larger crews, although to begin with the small crews could deal with each sail in turn.

There is one more find that ought to be mentioned. In the years 1971 to 1974 Polish archaeologists in the Bay of Gdansk (Danzig) were able to recover the remains of a carrack that had sunk there in the fifteenth century. Soon after the ship left harbour, having taken on a cargo of iron ore, pig-iron, copper, wax, timber and barrels of tar, fire must have broken out on board. The ship was clinker-built with an aftercastle and one mast. Unlike the Bremen cog, it was not flat-bottomed but had a profiled keel. The side-planks were riveted.

TECHNICAL ADVANCES IN MEDIEVAL SHIPBUILDING: THE CARVEL PLANKING METHOD

The motor behind progress in shipbuilding was the exchange of goods between different regions: Portuguese carracks sailed as far as English harbours, Hanseatic merchants travelled to Venice. In this way ship types from different regions came into contact with each other.

What is more, in 1492 Columbus had discovered the New World and the Portuguese were in the process of exploring the sea route around the Cape of Good Hope. The opening up of these long-distance seaways demanded continuous improvement in ship design. Alongside the lateen sail, a triangular sail set at an angle to the mast, Mediterranean seamen now took up the square-rigged, rectangular mainsail, which had long been used in the north, while northern boatbuilders adopted the carvel technique from the south. This method of construction would dominate wooden boat design into the modern era. The term is derived from the word *caravel*, a Portuguese design of ship, fitted with two or three masts and lateen sails.

From what we know of the history of seagoing ships in northern Europe, to start with, their hulls were mainly clinker-built and riveted. Not until after completion of the hull was it stiffened with cross-ribs. The cog was also built in this way, although the bottom-planks were fitted together flush.

The carvel technique was a decisive step forward since in this process each plank was separately fastened to the ribs in turn. This was done with wooden dowels. None other than Julius Caesar had encountered an early form of carvel building on the coasts of Brittany. The Portuguese used the technique for their caravels in the reign of Henry the Navigator. These ships had even stronger side-walls, with inner and outer planks mortised together. Furthermore, each cross-rib supported its own deck-beam. This meant that the deck could be made watertight where it joined the side-wall. Holes cut in the side-walls at deck height, called scuppers, allowed the sea water to run off.

In the course of the fifteenth century the more advanced carvel technique first reached the Netherlands, probably with Spanish and Portuguese ships, and from 1470 onwards it arrived in the Hanseatic cities of the Baltic. In 1446 the seamen of Bremen succeeded in capturing a carrack, though they considered it too misshapen, too high out of the water and fitted with too many masts. The first ships to be built in the north using the carvel technique were launched in 1460 in the Dutch ports of Hoorn and Zierikzee.

In 1464 the carvel ship *Peter van la Rochelle* was mortgaged in Danzig. This ship lay in harbour for a long time as the result of a prolonged legal wrangle with the city authorities. It had to be repaired to prevent it from sinking and hence became the property of the city. Rechristened *Peter von Danzig*, it was then referred to in the account of its captain, Councillor Berndt Pawest, as the *groote Kraveel* (the great caravel). With a length of 40 m and a crew of 400 men, the ship was one of the largest of its day.

The *Peter von Danzig* had three masts and was even able to beat to windward. Only the rudder-mounting gave frequent trouble. Around 1470 the Hanseatic city of Danzig adopted the carvel style for building its own ships.

Another Hanseatic city, Lübeck, owned a large carvel-built ship named the *Adler von Lübeck* (Eagle of Lübeck). Originally built as a warship, it was launched in 1566 and later converted to serve as a merchant-ship. The *Adler* was 65 m long and could carry 750 tonnes of cargo. Its rigging included, in addition to the now familiar fore-, main- and mizzen-masts, a further mast in the stern known as a 'bonaventure' mizzen. Below the bowsprit and support-ing it was a beak-shaped wooden structure. In 1581 the ship was

This engraving from 1480 shows a three-masted ship of carvel construction.

bound for Lisbon with a cargo of timber. However, on its return voyage with 1,600 barrels of salt, it sprang a leak and had to return to port, where it was sold and broken up.

PROSPECTS: AT THE THRESHOLD OF THE EARLY MODERN AGE

Until the first half of the sixteenth century the building of carvel-planked vessels became the norm. Only smaller coastal craft were still clinker-built. The new carvel technique made it possible to build bigger ships that were more watertight. With a stern-mounted rudder, three masts and a watertight deck, western Europe now possessed highly manoeuvrable and seaworthy ships. Long voyages could now be accomplished with the crew quartered in the fore- and aftercastles. All that remained was to make them defensible, since the invention of gunpowder had rendered crossbowmen obsolete. At first muskets were fixed to the walls of the 'castles', but this was not ideal. The problem was solved with gun-ports, which could be closed and made watertight when not in use. Behind these, on the lower deck, ship's cannons could be positioned. A ship of this kind is depicted for the first time on a seal from 1493, which had been commissioned by the Prefect of Burgundy, later the Emperor Maximilian.

From the early to the late Middle Ages shipbuilding on the North Sea and Baltic had progressed on a steep curve. From the Viking ships via the cog to the carrack, a variety of ships had plied the seas. With the growth of cities and the need for more and more goods, the foundations of an increasingly professionalised shipbuilding industry were laid in northern Europe. At the threshold of the Early Modern Age, with the inventions of the Spanish and Portuguese, innovations arrived from the Mediterranean world. Yet for a long time the cities of the Hansa clung to their old ships. Thus it was not until 1618 that in Lübeck the first *Fleute* was launched, a narrow-hulled, three-masted vessel that had been developed in the Netherlands at the end of the sixteenth century. Hanseatic shipbuilding then reached its final zenith in the mid-seventeenth century, with the big convoy ships carrying up to 54 cannon. The west now possessed a maritime weapon of war that was superior to any other type of ship in the world. In this way, a future of distant voyages of discovery and dominance of the world's oceans was secured. The basis for this had been provided by trading contacts which, since the early Middle Ages, had linked the coastal regions of the North Sea and the Baltic. But what was the use of better ships, if there were no progress in navigation as well?

3 FROM LANDMARKS TO CHARTS: ADVANCES IN NAVIGATION

EARLIEST AIDS TO NAVIGATION

When ships only sailed along coasts, sailors could navigate by landmarks. Only by a few dangerous shallows or at the mouths of rivers were there signal fires. At the entrance to the Divenow (now Dzwinów) Channel in modern Poland stood a brazier, mentioned by Adam of Bremen in the eleventh century, which guided ships up to the port of Wolin. Even the route taken by the Varangians along Russian rivers to the Black Sea, was lit in places by signal fires. For example, a signal tower has been excavated at Vitichev, 40 km south of Kiev. This had been erected in a castle rampart near an important river crossing. Not far from the bank of the Dnieper a tower on posts had been put up on an artificial mound. On the top platform of the tower a thick layer of earth had been laid, on which a hearth was placed. In the High Middle Ages a stone tower was built on the marshy island of Neuwerk at the entrance to the river Elbe. The tower had room for a crew and served as a landmark as well as a lighthouse.

However, once ships were out of sight of land, seamen had to be able to navigate across the open sea. On their voyages across the North Atlantic, the Vikings were the first people from northern Europe to achieve this. But without charts and any significant technical aids, how did they estimate their course? The position of the sun helped them to determine the points of the compass, but the swell, and the prevailing winds and currents in familiar waters also provided clues. At night, they could navigate by the stars, but off dangerous coasts with reefs and shallows they could only sail by day. Speed was estimated purely on the basis of experience in handling the ship. Cloud formations and flocks of birds had to be observed, as they were indicators of land beyond the horizon. These simple, empirical methods were used by seafarers over thousands of years: by the Phoenicians and Greeks in the Mediterranean, as well as by the Vikings in northern Europe. More complex navigational instruments were unknown until the introduction of the magnetic compass in the High Middle Ages. Only the lead-line, a long cord, knotted at intervals and with a lead weight at the end, was used to measure the depth of water. There is a scene in the Bayeux Tapestry depicting a crewman on the bow of a ship, swinging the lead.

Even so, the concept of sailing along a parallel of latitude must have been known to the Vikings; otherwise they could not have undertaken their long voyages across the North Atlantic. It is possible that the Norsemen possessed

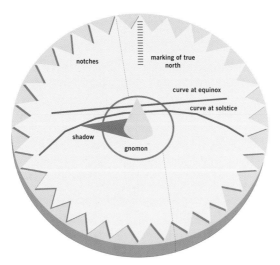

notches

marking of true north

curve at equinox

curve at solstice

shadow

gnomon

PRESERVED FRAGMENT
The Vikings' solar compass had notches round the edge to determine direction and a cone (the gnomon) in the centre, whose shadow showed the position of the sun.

some kind of simple solar compass, with which they could follow the apparent path of the sun from the eastern to the western horizon. Only the position of the sun at the zenith of its daily path, namely due south, remains unchanged. However, when the sun is not at its highest point, directions can only be roughly estimated.

The theory that the Vikings had a solar compass is based on a thousand-year-old broken disk of wood, found at a settlement in Greenland, the so-called East Settlement near the Uunartoq Fjord. Several years after its discovery, Captain C.V. Sølver recognised that the two lines engraved on the upper surface of the disk corresponded to the curves of a gnomon. These curves are the lines described by the shadow of a stick or cone (the gnomon or 'pointer' of a sundial) between sunrise and sunset. The trace of the curve varies according to the season and latitude. The two lines carved on the wooden disk – one straight and one curved – correspond to the course of the sun at the equinoxes and at the solstice. Originally the disk probably had a diameter of some 7 cm. The serrations cut into the circumference of the disk mark the 32 points of the compass. The gnomon was probably a small cone standing at the centre, at which there is a small hole. In order to calculate the heading of the ship, the navigator rotated the disk until the shadow of the gnomon fell exactly on the appropriate curve. The heading was then read off from the serrations on the outer edge.

ARABIAN NAVIGATION

Navigation in the Mediterranean and the Indian Ocean was far more advanced than in the north. It is possible that in the ninth and tenth centuries Arab seamen used a wooden pole or *kamal* to measure the elevation of the pole star above the horizon.

In addition, astrolabes were used to determine a ship's position by

As well as the astrolabe, there was also the nocturnal (sidereal clock). It consisted of two concentric circles of different sizes, of wood or brass, one superimposed on the other. The lower disc, with a handle, was divided into twelve sections to represent the months of the year, the upper one into twenty-four, representing the hours. The central hole was aimed at the Pole Star, and calibration of the pointer on an imaginary line connecting two stars in Ursa Major or Minor allowed the user to calculate the time at night.

reference to heavenly bodies. These instruments consisted of a horizontal ring marked out in degrees up to 360, and a vertical quadrant with a movable arm, which was fixed but rotatable within the ring. After aligning the ring with the horizon, the elevation (azimuth) of every heavenly body could be measured by aiming the arm on the quadrant at it. The astrolabe was probably first used by the Greek astronomer Hipparchus, in the 2nd century BC. Until the introduction of the sextant in the eighteenth century, small astrolabes were the principal instruments of navigation.

The Arabs had not only benefited from the heritage of the ancient world, but had made further advances in mathematics and, through practical experiments, in navigation. In order to determine the hours for prayer it had been important to measure the length of shadows at midday. However, this measurement is dependent on the sun's elevation and the geographical latitude. In order to calculate the varying length of shadow cast, the Caliph al-Mamoun (AD 813–33, or 198–218 in Arabic chronology) ordered the carrying out of exact measurements of the annual movement of the sun in Baghdad and on Mount Qasiyn near Damascus. As well as the astrolabe, geometric compasses and clocks were used, and also highly detailed tables, called *zidj*, which gave astronomical values and trigonometric functions.

By means of astronomical observations of the sun's position the degree of latitude could be determined, though not yet the degree of longitude. Even explorers of the modern age still had to contend with that problem. Before then, sailors had to use pilot-books, sailing directions and the experience of skilled navigators to get round the difficulty. The Portuguese seafarer and explorer Vasco da Gama, for example, had an Arab navigator on board his ship.

SAILING DIRECTIONS AND THE COMPASS

In medieval northern Europe the other principal aid was provided by sailing directions. The earliest evidence of this is contained in the accounts of voyages, already mentioned, made by Ottar the Norwegian and Wulfstan the Englishman, from the Norwegian coast southwards to Hedeby and from there to Truso and the southern coast of the Baltic. The sailing directions, which the Hanseatic sailors also used, contained directional information from quadrants, the forerunners of the sextant. The duration of the voyage was given, but no distances or landmarks. In 1578, when the envoy of Philip II of Spain, Francisco de Eraso, sailed from Stralsund to Kalmar in south-east Sweden, he complained to his patron not only about the uneatable food and the poor state of the ship, but most of all about the terrifying style of navigation: the Baltic shipmasters, he wrote, had neither charts nor compass, but steered according to a little book. A hundred and fifty years earlier, Fra Maro had noted on his famous world map of 1428 that people did not sail by chart or compass, but by the lead-line.

The 'little book' mentioned by Francisco de Eraso contained sailing directions. In Hamburg's Commerzbibliothek (Library of Commerce), two bound volumes, the *Seebuch* (Sea-Book) of c. 1470, can still be seen. The best-preserved historical source of Hanseatic navigation, it contains sailing directions for voyages from the Atlantic coast to Russia, and covers the entire North Sea and Baltic. However, since both Norway and the German port of Lübeck are missing, the book probably originated in Flanders. From the very precise sailing directions, we can glean measured distances, compass courses, soundings and leading-marks. For the passage through the Öresund, between Denmark and Sweden, we read the following:

Item when Skagen reef is past, and you have 14 fathoms with a soft bottom, head southwards, on no other course, for as long as Læso lies north-east of you; then head south-east, until you are into ten fathoms, cast the lead until the church of Helsinør and the bake-house [a building that must have since disappeared] lie so that you can see between them; in that way you cannot fail to sail the correct course for Lappesand in 7 fathoms.

Islands were a very important feature in sailing directions. Thus from the island of Gotland, for example, courses radiate out in all directions, like maritime highways to different ports. On these courses, ships could remain *upp der trade* (Low German for 'on course') or *upp den richtschen trat* ('on the correct course'). If he wandered off the prescribed course the shipmaster did all he could to find his way back on to it, even if that meant having to make a wide detour. Just like sailors in the Viking age, those of the Hansa had to take repeated soundings.

Along the coast, assistance was given by natural features of the coastline – hills, estuaries and clumps of trees – as well as man-made structures such as church spires and lighthouses or other navigational marks erected for shipping. Initially the entrances to harbours were marked, as for example by the Travemünde Tower built in 1226. From the fourteenth century onwards, the custom of illuminating these marks with fires probably spread from Flanders to the other coasts of northern Europe. In 1316 we have the first mention of a lighthouse-keeper, the *custos lucernae*, in Travemünde. The marking of navigable channels with barrels, or buoys, also spread from the tidal waters of the Dutch and Flemish coasts. There are records of these in the rivers Vlie, Maas and Marsdiep as early as the fourteenth century. Since the shipmasters were not familiar with every sea area, they would recruit crewmen with the necessary experience.

The next step in the improvement of navigation was the development of a serviceable magnetic compass. The compass had already been known in ancient China and probably reached the Arabs from there. Around 1200 we have the first evidence of its use in the English Channel, then a century later it was adopted by the Scandinavians. It is first mentioned in the North Sea in 1433, and in the Baltic in 1460. The practical value to navigation of these very simple, early instruments is often overestimated. Since seamen in those days did not realise that the presence of iron in ships could lead to large compass errors, the course indicated often led to disaster. Thus, despite a certain amount of progress, seafaring still remained a very risky business. Many ships failed to reach their destination, and they often ran aground a short distance from harbour, since there were no reliable charts showing the location of reefs and shallows.

THE FIRST CHARTS

Navigation in tidal waters was particular dangerous, with the strong ebb and flood and the constantly shifting channels. So, not surprisingly, it was in these waters that the first charts in northern Europe were created. Owing to the lack of knowledge of surveying techniques, the charts that appeared in the sixteenth century were very inexact. At first they were no more than illustrations of the sailing directions and should not be equated with modern hydrographic charts.

Only much later came detailed charts of sections of coastline, which supplemented the sailing directions but did not replace them. This meant that, at first, the north European charts did not achieve the same level of importance as the Portolan or Periplus charts that circulated in the Mediterranean region. On to those charts their Italian and Catalan cartographers had drawn numerous compass bearings as aids for setting a course towards particular ports. Taking these as his model, the Dutchman Cornelis Anthoniszoon drew his *Caerte von Ostland* in the middle of the sixteenth century. But even on this chart the coastline and offshore islands of the North Sea coast were represented in a simplified fashion. As late as the 1580s the city of Amsterdam commissioned a nautical expert to sail along and chart the North Sea coast of Schleswig-Holstein, the detail of which was still unknown.

The large-format atlas entitled *Spieghel van de Zeevaerdt* (Mirror of Navigation), published in Leiden in 1584 or 1585 by Lucas Janszoon

Waghenaer, represented a decisive step forward. Waghenaer was born in 1534 at Enkhuizen, a port on the Zuider Zee (which is now largely drained and renamed the Ijsselmeer), and spent several years at sea as a pilot and navigator. In addition to numerous charts, his atlas contained a description of the important stretches of coast and shipping routes from southern Spain to Norway and the Baltic.

A chart devoted specifically to the coast of Schleswig-Holstein was produced in 1620 by an anonymous cartographer. It shows the Eider estuary, which, since 1973 has been closed off by a causeway, the Eiderdamm, with a lock for small vessels. On the chart we can recognise the fairway of the Outer Eider, with all its shallows, sandbanks and channels, as well as its buoys and other navigation marks. There are sailing-directions for setting course out of the estuary westwards to the island of Heligoland, and upstream to the 'newly built town on the Eyder', the present-day Friedrichstadt.

Until the Early Modern Age, charts remained no more than a supplement to the sailing directions. The first genuinely serviceable chart covering the German Bight and the marshy Friesian and Schleswig coasts was produced

In order to gauge the depth of the water and hence, to some extent, position and course, soundings were constantly taken in coastal waters.

in 1708–10 by Capt. Mathurin Guitet under commission from the Dutch Admiralty. For at least ten years Guitet had piloted convoys of merchant ships down the Weser from Bremen, around the shallow and treacherous German coast and up the Elbe to Hamburg. On the other hand, his otherwise exemplary chart gives an inadequate description of the west coast of Schleswig-Holstein, from the mouth of the Elbe north to the Eider estuary, since Guitet clearly had no knowledge of this sea area.

The improvements both in navigation and shipbuilding thus provided the foundations upon which maritime trade could expand. After a long period of reliance on empirical experience, charts and the fixing of positions became increasingly precise.

LITIGATION CHARTS

We also have an early representation of the river Elbe in chart form. However, the Elbe chart of Melchior Lorich is not a navigational chart in the real sense, but a chart for use in litigation, in order to establish in a court of law the boundaries of the fairways or shipping channels. Since the mid-sixteenth century the Hanseatic city of Hamburg had been pursuing actions before the Imperial Court against Duke Otto von Harburg and against the riparian towns of Lüneburg, Stade and Buxtehude. The Hanseatic city wanted to impose a toll on all ships coming up the Elbe. During the trial, Hamburg astonished its opponents by producing a newly drawn chart of the Elbe, some 12 m long, in order to demonstrate the precise width of the shipping channel on the lower Elbe. Furthermore, the men of Hamburg used the chart to emphasise the care they devoted to providing buoys and beacons for the safety of shipping. With a precision rare for that time, the chart also reproduces the land on either side of the channel, with its landscape and topographical features.

Other litigation charts, albeit far less detailed, show manmade water-ways, such as the Alster–Beste Canal. Built between 1525 and 1529, with permission from the Danish king Frederic I, the canal partially used the river Trave to link the Hanseatic cities of Hamburg and Lübeck. This provided a direct connection between the two ports and thus between the North Sea and the Baltic. No sooner was the waterway completed than a dispute over tolls arose here as well, between Hamburg and the Duke of Lauenburg. The chart produced in duplicate by Hamburg on 21 October 1528 is the oldest hand-drawn map of Schleswig-Holstein.

However, these litigation charts were not intended for seamen. They were only 'one-offs' because, until the improvement of printing technology, all charts were drawn by hand and thus remained rare and costly.

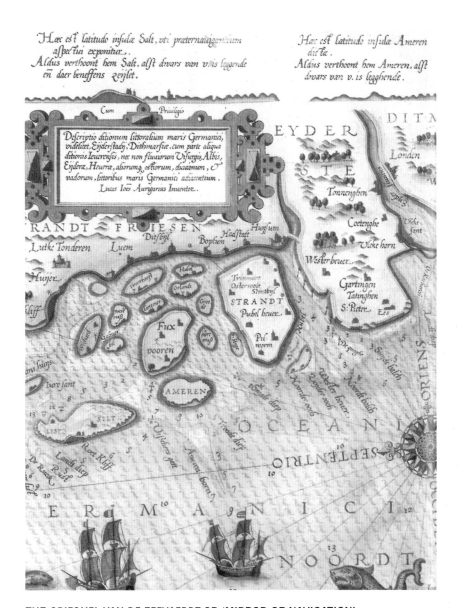

THE *SPIEGHEL VAN DE ZEEVAERDT* OR 'MIRROR OF NAVIGATION'

This section of a chart from the second volume of the *Spieghel van de Zeevaerdt* by Lucas Janszoon Waghenaer shows the North Sea coast of Schleswig-Holstein. We can see the marshy coastline of northern Friesland, though the chart should be rotated 90 degrees to the right, since the coast runs roughly north–south. In a great storm in 1634, the large island named Strandt in the centre of the chart was split into two; these parts are now called Pellworm and Nordstrand. The chart shows the main fairways with depths marked in fathoms, as well as shallows, sea marshes and navigation-marks. The outlines of the islands and mainland coast are highly schematic, but the landward features visible from the sea are clearly marked. The inland areas, of no great interest to seafarers, have been left blank, and precedence is clearly given to the navigational routes and the landward view from the sea. Round the edge of the map there are views of the coast as they appear to the sailor. These realistically drawn views had to be reliable, since they were intended to be compared with the actual coastline for the purposes of orientation. The various compass bearings are a further aid to navigation.

DORESTAD, LONDON, RIBE: THE NORTH SEA AND ITS EARLY TRADING PORTS

THE NORTH SEA

The lands around the North Sea – England, Scotland, the Netherlands, Germany, Denmark and Norway – display a great variety of coastlines and shores. The geology has been shaped by the rise in the sea level at the end of the last Ice Age. During that era much of what is now the North Sea consisted of flat sandy plains. England was not yet separated from continental Europe by the Channel. As a result of the warming of the climate, the glaciers melted and the sea flooded the flat plains. Some 6,500 to 7,000 years ago the North Sea reached the edge of the moraines, the deposits left by the last Ice Age but one, in the Netherlands, north-west Germany and Denmark.

Since that time, however, the coastlines have undergone further great changes, chiefly along the southern coast of the North Sea. Along the edge of this shallow sea extensive sea marshes and mudflats have formed, criss-crossed by creeks and channels, and to seaward, constantly shifting sandbanks and sandbars. Until the building of dykes from the High Middle Ages onwards, the marshes were regularly flooded at exceptionally high tides. The impact of storms created new bays and inlets, while elsewhere arms of the sea silted up. It was the southern coast of the North Sea in particular – from the estuaries of the Rhine, Maas, Ijssel and Scheldt in the south, up to the Ems, Elbe and Eider – that was constantly exposed to these modifications, to which shipping had to adapt. By contrast, much of the east coasts of Scotland and northern England, as well as the cliffs and fjords of Norway, shelved more steeply, as did the south coast of England, from the white cliffs of Dover, westward. The only opportunities for building harbours here were on the estuaries and fjords that penetrated deep inland.

In the early Middle Ages trade developed between these various ports, in which the Friesians, Franks, Anglo-Saxons and Norsemen all participated. From Dorestad in the Rhine delta shipping routes radiated westward to London, and into the Irish Sea, north to Ribe in western Denmark, and finally round Jutland and through the Danish islands to Hedeby in Schleswig. We have archaeological and historical evidence of life in these early mercantile settlements and their harbours, and of the commerce in goods around the North Sea.

Even in Roman times the Rhine provided an important link between the province of Britannia and the coastal areas settled by Friesians. At the same time the river formed the north-eastern frontier of the Roman empire. Two towns in this region, *Forum Hadriani*, near today's Dutch capital, The Hague (Den Haag), and *Noviomagus*, modern Nijmegen, both had estimated populations of about 5,000. Also in the areas near the river, military *vici* existed to serve Roman frontier forts or *castella*.

With the end of Roman rule, this system of settlements collapsed. In the fourth and fifth centuries AD, Germanic tribes, chiefly Friesians and Franks, swarmed across the Rhine in increasing numbers. According to Tacitus in his *Germania* (Bk III), the Friesians originally occupied an area between the right (eastern) bank of the Rhine, the North Sea and an inland sea that he called *Lacus Flevo*, the early forerunner of the Zuider Zee, which, since its partial drainage has become the Ijsselmeer. Several centuries later, an English historian, the Venerable Bede, identified the *Fresones* (Friesians), *antiqui Saxones* (ancient Saxons) and the *Boructarii* (a Frankish tribe, also called the *Bructi*), as neighbouring tribes. From as early as the second half of the third century AD there had been close ties between the Franks and the Saxons. Like the Friesians, both these peoples were described as pirates when they launched marauding expeditions along the coast of Roman Gaul in the years AD 285–286. However, the fact is that after the withdrawal of the Roman armies at the turn of the fourth and fifth centuries, the entire Rhine delta, and with it the coastal region of the Netherlands, fell under the control of the Friesians.

Even during the troubled period of mass westward migration, traffic along the Rhine never entirely came to a halt. The Friesians and Franks who had seized the lands at the mouth of the Rhine recognised the value of this waterway. It was for this reason that in the seventh and eighth centuries, long after the Romans had gone, the Rhine delta became a bone of contention between the Friesians and Franks. The Franks made repeated attempts to gain ascendancy over the area, since they knew its economic and strategic value. Even today, the estuaries of the Rhine, Maas and Scheldt are among the world's most important commercial gateways. Rotterdam and Europoort comprise the world's largest seaport, while other big cities like Antwerp and Amsterdam lie within the delta region.

In the Dark Ages, the Old Rhine entered the North Sea further north than today, near the former Roman frontier fort of Valkenburg (near Leiden), where it breached a line of dunes running north and south. Later on, this estuary silted up. If seamen followed the Old or 'Crooked' Rhine inland, they entered a region of marshland, which extended back from the raised riverbanks. In the early Middle Ages the destination for these ships was the trading settlement of Dorestad at the intersection of two important trading routes. For it is here that the lower Rhine is joined by the Crooked Rhine (*Kromme Rijn* in Dutch) and becomes the Lek. Further south, the Lek joins the Maas, or Meuse, which flows from northern France into the North Sea. The broad delta formed by these rivers was known by the Romans as *Helinium*. South of the Maas, the marshlands continued as far as the estuary of the Scheldt.

The whole landscape of *Friesia Magna* was characterised by the sea, and by lakes, rivers and tidal creeks, lying between large expanses of bog and marshland. That is why craft of all sizes were the most important means of transport. However, we know little about the degree of mobility and the social structures that bound this maritime race together. That is why the archaeological finds in Dorestad, the largest settlement in the region, are so important.

Dorestad, the meeting point between Friesians and Franks

With Dorestad, on the Crooked Rhine not far from modern Utrecht, the Friesians had founded an important centre for long-distance trade. The settlement lay at the point where the course of the Rhine divides into the Crooked Rhine and the Lek. The ancient heart of Dorestad, dating from the seventh century, is probably at the same location as the Roman *Castellum Levafanum*, marked on a Roman map, and which was later washed away by the river Lek. From there the focus of settlement shifted further north. At that time Dorestad was situated on the frontier of the former Merovingian realm, and came alternately under Friesian and Frankish domination.

In AD 690 Pippin II, the Frankish 'Mayor of Austrasia', began a series of military offensives, which ended the independence of the Friesian elite in Dorestad. In 695 the Friesian leader, Radbod, finally bowed to Frankish power. Between 688 and 720 Friesland was conquered as far as the river Vlie, and by 734 all the Friesian towns as far as the river Lauwers, in central Holland, had fallen under Frankish control. Dorestad now grew to become the region's most important Frankish stronghold. In 695, Pippin II, who now ruled Friesland south of the Rhine, established a bishopric in Utrecht to which he appointed the Northumbrian missionary, Willibrord. From this point on, a systematic network of government was established by Frankish troops, Anglo-Saxon missionaries and new settlers, referred to as *homines Franci* in contemporary sources. It is true that there were uprisings in the years that followed, but these had little impact on the domination of the Franks over the Rhine delta.

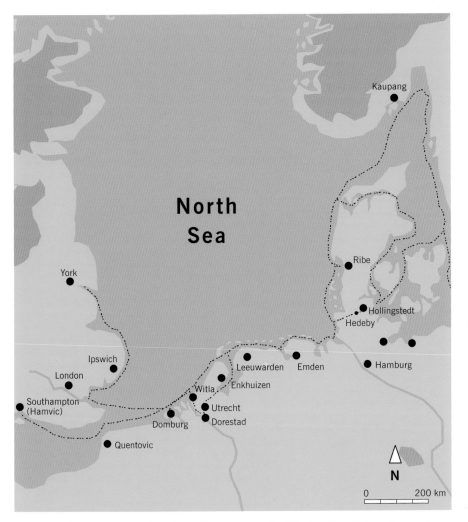

From AD 700 onwards, trading ships plied between the Friesian–Frankish trading centre of Dorestad, and ports in England, Scandinavia and along the coast of Holland and Germany.

If Dorestad had become a point of conflict between Friesians and Franks, then it was not so much because of its role as the Friesian capital as by reason of its port, which in the course of the seventh century had become the principal clearing-house between the hinterland of the Rhine and Moselle on one hand, and England and Scandinavia on the other. Natural and agricultural products, volcanic tufa, timber, corn, and wine; ceramics, glass and weaponry made by Rhenish craftsmen; metals, leather, fur and amber from Scandinavia, not to mention slaves – were all traded here. Thus Friesian trade was not restricted to supplying inland markets, and exporting its own produce, but it was also an entrepôt for trade between many different regions. Thanks to the Frankish conquest of Dorestad, what was originally just a Friesian affair became Frankish–Friesian commerce. Revenues from customs tariffs flowed into the Merovingian and Carolingian treasuries. From the time of Pippin II and Charlemagne, if not earlier, a customs regime was in operation, which supervised shipping traffic and imposed taxes.

In addition, Dorestad was the site of the most productive mint in the entire Frankish empire. The first Frankish coins had been struck there as early as AD 635, and around 650 the Merovingian mint-master, Madelinus, was resident in the city. These coins, the *trientes* and later the *denarii*, circulated widely in Friesland, Groningen and Zeeland. In order to satisfy the demand for gold coinage, Dorestad also minted its own coin, the Donrijp. In the Carolingian period the Dorestad mint shared in the production of *sceattas*. From the distribution of finds of these coins, we are not only able to deduce the trade routes, but, for the first time, the names then given to the city of their origin: *Dorestate*, *Dorestat* or *Dorestado*.

Dorestad in historical sources

The growth of the city was in fact a direct consequence of its integration in the Frankish empire, since this made it easier for Friesian merchants to gain access to the interior. The nearby episcopal seat of Utrecht also favoured the development of Dorestad. The port's function as the entrepôt for Frankish–Friesian trade from the Rhine delta to England, northern Europe and Scandinavia is confirmed by written sources as well as archaeological finds. In about 800, Dorestad is named by the missionary to the Friesians, Liudger, as a *vicus famosus* and in 834 as *vicus nominatissimus* ('a town of very great repute'). In Charlemagne's day, Dorestad is mentioned as the starting-point for crossings to England, and in 826 as a stage on the route to Scandinavia. Further accounts bear witness to the presence of Scandinavian merchants from Birka in central Sweden, and other Baltic centres. These men could not have reached Dorestad except by sea. Even in Italy, the Cosmographer of Ravenna, in his description of the known world from about AD 700, mentions a town he calls *Dorestate* in the Rhine delta, in the land of the Friesians. Even though Dorestad was abandoned at the end of the ninth century, its name has been preserved in the nearby Dutch village of Wijk bij Duurstede.

The significance of the place is shown by the presence of royal authority. Thus written sources tell us that in the ninth century royal officials were empowered to raise revenues from tolls as well as from the mint and from courts of law. The Bishop of Utrecht also had influence over Dorestad. The

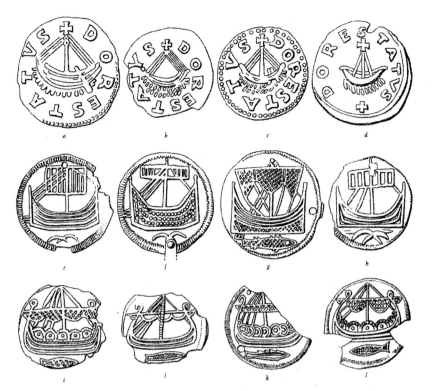

On these Carolingian coins we see not only the name of Dorestad (*Dorestatus*) but also vessels, one of which carries a cross at its masthead as a sign of peaceful trading.

many written sources suggest that the settlement extended over a considerable area and boasted a substantial population. The different terms used to identify it, namely *castrum* (fortification), *emporium* (trading settlement), *portus* (harbour) and *vicus* (town), indicate its varied aspects.

Archaeological finds from excavations in 1967 and 1977 indicate a prosperous town, but also reveal the reason why it was abandoned: the shift in the course of the river.

The harbour and the changing course of the river

In the early Middle Ages the Crooked Rhine ran east of what is today the main street of Wijk bij Duurstede. There it is still possible to see that in those days the river made a large meander or loop, until it was enclosed by dykes in 1122. Here, the left bank of the river initially followed the gentle curve of the road. During the period when Dorestad was inhabited, the course of the river shifted further to the east. A gently sloping beach developed on the inner side of the constantly widening meander.

Excavations on the main street of Wijk have revealed part of the northern

At the confluence of the Crooked Rhine (Dutch: *Kromme Rijn*) and the Lek the trading centre of Dorestad grew up in the seventh century near the present-day village of Wijk bij Duurstede.

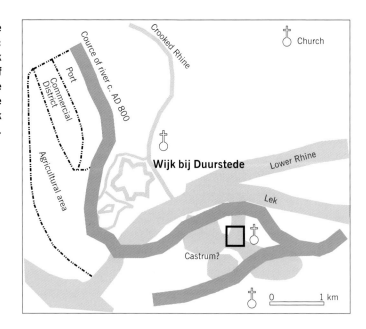

harbour area from the early medieval period. They show that when the harbour was first in operation it adjoined the river immediately west of it. The low sandy shore made it possible to beach the ships. and this was probably the single most important factor behind the founding of the settlement on this site. However, as the river shifted its course eastwards, a marshy depression formed, which was bridged by wooden jetties, in order to facilitate the continued loading and unloading of ships. The further the watercourse moved, the longer were the jetties that extended out into the riverbed. The earliest jetties were built in the late seventh century and the latest after AD 725. In the ninth century the construction activities appear to have come to an end. The jetties in the area of the present-day main street had now reached a length of up to 200 metres. The costly construction of these extended jetties shows the efforts that were made to maintain the once favoured port and trading centre. Even quite large ships were able to moor at these wooden piers.

The settlement

Goods were transported from the ships along the jetties to the settlement beyond. Archaeology reveals to us how the trading-settlement developed. It comprised two sections: one was a densely built mercantile quarter, running for about 3 km along the river, and back from the bank for a distance of 100 to 300 m; beyond that was a more sparsely built township. The mercantile quarter was divided into narrow plots running down at right angles to the river bank, forming a close-packed complex. On the adjacent plots stood small buildings. The main street ran through the mercantile zone, parallel to the river, and several other streets crossed the area at right angles. On the landward side (in what is today called *De Heul*), there were large farms in the early Middle Ages, which provided food for the community. Not far away, the inhabitants laid their dead to rest in a large cemetery. Presumably there was also a wooden church there. A second focus of settlement, as yet scarcely investigated, may have been situated on the peninsula between the Lek and the Rhine, the former site of a Roman *castellum*. It is possible that at this point both banks of the river were used for mooring.

We can only make a rough estimate of Dorestad's population at between 1,000 and 2,000 people. They were involved in farming, commerce and artisan trades. Agriculture, to cater for the merchants, travellers and administrators, was carried on in the township itself and in the surrounding land. The farm produce could be exchanged for craft wares and other goods. Archaeological finds show that the inhabitants wove textiles, made combs from horn, practised stonemasonry and glass-blowing, fashioned articles from wood and probably also built ships. We can assume that specialised artisans were resident in the waterfront district, possibly working in the service of the owners of the plots. However, what Dorestad essentially lived on was sea-borne trade. This is shown by the numerous imports, such as large quantities of Rhenish potteries: the so-called 'Pingsdorf Ware', and amphorae with bands of bas-relief round them, which were produced near the present-day town of Brühl, on the Rhine between Cologne and Bonn. In addition to these there were 'Tating Jugs', polished black wine flasks decorated with tin-foil. The spread of Tating Jugs extends from the Rhine delta to eastern England, south and central Scandinavia, Norway and as far as Lake Ladoga, where St Petersburg now stands. This distribution is also true of certain types of glassware, which graced noble tables of the period.

Given its great importance as a trading centre, it is no surprise that Dorestad was closely supervised by the successive Carolingian monarchs of the period and to some extent by the Church. From the burial finds in Dorestad, we get no clear idea of the part played by the Friesians in this early medieval long-distance trade. Were they the inhabitants of the riverside quarter in the northern port area? Were they free men or servants of the nobility or the Church? At all events the active radius of their merchant ships reached as far as Ribe in Jutland, and occasionally even to the Baltic coasts occupied by Scandinavians and Slavs.

The picture described here relates to a period from the late seventh to the mid-ninth century. During this time we can be sure that the town went through considerable change. For whereas, in the seventh century, Dorestad lay on the fringe of the lands ruled by the late Merovingians, in the Carolingian period it was well within the borders of the empire.

The end of Dorestad

The causes of the decline and disappearance of this early town can be found in a combination of several factors. From as early as the second quarter of the ninth century it went into economic decline. The disputes within the empire and the collapse of political unity at the end of the reign of Ludwig the Pious hastened this trend. From as early as 834, before the end of Ludwig's reign, Norman raiders had terrorised the coastal regions. The Franks could put up little resistance to sudden seaborne assaults. The extent of their helplessness is shown by the fact that from 839 to 841 Dorestad was temporarily ceded to the Norman leader, Rorik. He made it his seat of power, but was now in fact the representative of Frankish royal authority, and had to take on the task of repelling Norman incursions. Thus peace reigned for a time. Yet by 836 Dorestad was again subject to heavy attacks by the Normans and was finally destroyed. Many Friesian merchants lost their lives. The town disappeared from historical record. Dorestad's place was taken by towns like Deventer and Tiel. Indeed, the Bishop of Utrecht had retreated to Deventer, since he wanted to keep control of the burgeoning trade there.

The retreat of royal and episcopal power thus had far-reaching consequences for Dorestad. Other early medieval trading ports, like Ghent and Antwerp, which became the seats of bishops or princes, went on to grow into major cities in the High Middle Ages. Not so Dorestad. For here another factor came into play, which sealed the fate of the port: the old course of the Rhine increasingly silted up, not least because the original mouth became blocked by a sand bar. Thus Dorestad now lay on a dead end; shipping moved to the estuaries of the Maas and the Scheldt.

THE ENGLISH CHANNEL, THAMES AND HUMBER

From the Rhine/Maas/Scheldt delta, maritime trade routes led to England. On the island of Walcheren (then called *Walacria*) stood the trading town of Domburg, some distance from a port that already existed in Roman times. Since the old shoreline has been washed away, little can be said about the medieval entrepôt. It is probable that in its heyday in the sixth and seventh centuries, a mercantile settlement extended for a long way parallel with the shore.

From Domburg, Quentovic (in Normandy) and Witla (in the Vlaardingen district of Rotterdam), ships sailed along the coast to Calais and then made the short crossing over the Channel to Hamwic (today Southampton) on the south coast of England. Another way of reaching London and Hamwic once existed from Dorestad via Utrecht on the Old Rhine. As already explained, the mouth of the Rhine then lay further north than today. At times it was even safe to cross the Channel by night – usually from northern France – since from 811 a fire-beacon at Boulogne showed the way. The chief destinations in England were four important ports, which all lay at the mouths of rivers and were important for the defence of the regional kingdoms that were emerging there: Hamwic for Wessex, London for Mercia, Ipswich for East Anglia and York for Northumbria.

Hamwic–Southampton

The trading settlement of Hamwic was founded soon after AD 700 on the west bank of the river Itchen, which flows into Southampton Water; that in turn joins the Solent, the straits between the Isle of Wight and the mainland, and thence reaches the English Channel. It is described in early sources as a *mercimonium*, a market, and may have been built on royal lands. To date only 3 per cent of the 45-hectare settlement area has been excavated. Owing to the presence of the busy modern port, it has not been possible to uncover the presumed ancient wharves on the west bank of the Itchen. Streets surfaced with gravel crossed the township of small wooden houses, which was surrounded by a ditch. From 720, and possibly earlier, *sceattas* were minted in Hamwic as a trading currency. In addition to commerce, the inhabitants of Hamwic made their living from various craft activities such as glass-blowing, textile-weaving and pottery. Since far more men than women were buried in the surrounding fields, we may assume that the resident community was exclusively devoted to commerce and trades that benefited from the town's maritime links.

Lundenburth–Lundenwic–London

From Quentovic in Normandy, ships could not only sail to Hamwic, but also take an S-shaped course along the coast of Kent, to a port of call west of Dover and from there round the North Foreland and into the wide Thames estuary. The vessels then sailed some 60 miles (100 km) up to London in the kingdom of Mercia. The wharves of Roman Londinium had fallen into disrepair and so a new commercial port was established a little way downstream. Even so, the former city centre was not entirely abandoned, for it was here, probably on land where St Paul's Cathedral now stands, that the bishop had his seat. In order to distinguish the older Roman city from the new trading centre, the former was named Lundenburth. The trading settlement established immediately west of the stone walls, on the banks of the Fleet, a tributary of the Thames, was named Lundenwic. Through this quarter, parallel to the Thames, ran a street, still called The Strand, which now leads to Trafalgar Square. Bordered by the river on its south side, the trading district was surrounded by a rampart to the north. Its gravel streets were lined with wooden houses. Upstream, the Thames bends south, and where Westminster now stands there was an island.

Finds of imported ceramics and grindstones point to trading contacts with northern France and, less intensively, with the Friesian coast and the Rhineland. As in Hamwic, many signs have been found of commercial production in London. Later, when London was threatened by Viking raiders and finally captured, the majority of the population of Lundenwic moved to neighbouring Lundenburth.

Ipswich

From the Thames ships headed out into the North Sea and could sail further up the east coast of England. In Suffolk, the river Orwell led up to the port of Ipswich. On the north side of the river there were wooden piles shoring up the bank, to which ships could tie up. Beyond lay a settlement of some 7 hectares in area. Unlike the other trading settlements founded in the seventh century, Ipswich was not abandoned in the ninth century but has remained in existence as a port, virtually without interruption, until the present day.

Eburacum–Eoforwic–York

Further up the English coast, ships finally reached the wide Humber estuary, the second largest gateway to England. Sailing up the Humber and then the Ouse, the ships came to a city that had since Roman times been the most important military and administrative centre in northern England, York. Near the former Roman military base of Eboracum, and only separated from it by the river, lay the early medieval trading settlement of Eoforwic. Within the bounds of the military base was the seat of the bishopric. The fortified civilian town attached to it, the *colonia*, lay opposite on the south bank of the Ouse. Since the harbour district of Anglo-Saxon York has not yet been excavated, we have no information about the wharves of that period. However, we can be sure that from the second half of the eighth century Friesians plied the sea routes to the Thames and Humber, as is shown, for example, by the Friesian combs that have been found.

The apprentice pieces (right) testify to the work of craftsmen in the Viking settlement of Dublin, while the 'Tating' jugs (below) show that ceramics from the Rhineland had spread as far as Sweden.

Ireland and the Irish Sea

Between England and Ireland lies the Irish Sea. From Europe this can be approached by two sea routes: either from the south, down the English Channel and round Land's End, or round the north of Scotland and down through the Western Isles. Ships taking the latter route in the early Middle Ages laid a course from the Hebrides to the Isle of Man and thence reached Dublin. The Isle of Man grew into an important port of call on the trading route to Dublin.

The Norsemen were attracted to Dublin because it was sited on an important ford across the river Liffey. We know that a settlement was established there by the Vikings in AD 841, but so far there is no archaeological evidence of it. After the Norsemen had been driven out from there, they returned in about 917 and founded a trading post where Dublin now stands. Archaeological excavations in the boggy soil beneath Fishamble Street have revealed several plots of land bounded by wicker fences, with small dwelling houses and outhouses. Tracks made from baulks of timber crossed the township. Crafts were carried on in many of the houses. During the tenth century Dublin became a prosperous city, as did other ports on the Irish Sea such as Chester and Bristol. The Norse rulers of Dublin, having grown rich from trade, rapidly expanded their power over the Irish Sea, captured the Isle of Man and seized the kingdom of York from the Danes, holding it until 952. However, in the years that followed, quarrels among the Vikings in Ireland itself led to the loss of their supremacy.

THE COASTAL WETLANDS BETWEEN THE RHINE AND EIDER ESTUARIES

From Dorestad, ships had a choice of routes: either round the coast of northern Holland, with its treacherous sandbanks, or along the less dangerous river route, along the Crooked Rhine to Utrecht and thence along the Vecht to what was then an inland sea, known as the Almere, later renamed the Zuider Zee. Along the edge of the Almere were the trading ports of Muiden and Medemblik in northern Holland and Staveren in Westergo. Through the marshy river Vlie there was a connection to the North Sea. But here the terrain was in a constant state of change.

Lacus Flevo–Almere–Zuider Zee–Ijsselmeer

In Roman times, the area that is now the Ijsselmeer was an inland freshwater lake fringed with marshes, the *Lacus Flevo*, which was only connected to the North Sea by narrow creeks. Around AD 800, as a result of storm-driven floods, the narrow creeks became so wide that the freshwater lake turned into the brackish Almere. In subsequent storms the creeks widened still further, so that by the late Middle Ages the salty Zuider Zee was formed, with a wide opening to the sea. The building of a huge dam, the Afsluitdijk, in the 1930s created the Ijsselmeer that we know today; much of it has been drained to provide rich farmland.

Leeuwarden in western Friesland

In the early Middle Ages the tidal river Vlie flowed from the Almere northwestwards to the sea. The storm-floods of the late Middle Ages completely transformed the coastal landscape with its marshy islands. From the Almere the sea route went north-west along the wetland coast of northern Holland. The coastline behind the islands and sandbanks possessed the same advantage as the Scandinavian skerries, namely that even with a strong wind blowing out at sea, the coastal waters remained a great deal calmer. Using wide inlets and estuaries, ships could sail from the Friesian coast a long way inland. One of these inlets (now dried out) was created as earlier as Roman times. Known as the *Middelzee*, it widened considerably in the early Middle Ages, and made it possible to take a ship as far as the town of Leeuwarden (today many miles inland from the North Sea and the Ijsselmeer). The origins of Leeuwarden lay in a hamlet called Wurt, on the eastern shore of the Middelzee, comprising a church and some farmhouses built on an artificial hill as protection from flooding. Later, in the eleventh and twelfth centuries, two more elongated '*wurts*' were raised, on which stood a trading settlement. The three hills merged in the late Middle Ages to form the town of Leeuwarden.

Eastern Friesland, Emden

If ships sailed into the Ems, whose estuary was narrower than it is today, before the sea broke in to form the wide Dollart bight, they would reach the port of Emden. In the early Middle Ages a single-street village grew up as a trading post on the eastern embankment of the Ems. The township was further from the coast than it is today, and was situated in a sheltered riverside position near the mouth of a tributary, the Ehe. At the intersection of sea routes and waterways running into the hinterland, Emden was thus well placed to become an entrepôt for Frankish–Friesian North Sea trade. In the eleventh century, as an important link to the North Sea, the river Ems was – according to the 17 Friesian land-laws – one of the four waterways serving the interior that enjoyed royal protection. The same source also names three highways under royal protection, one of which ran beside the Ems and linked Emden with the episcopal seat of Münster.

Archaeological excavations carried out between 1951 and 1959 show that oldest core of the town, dating from the eighth or ninth century, lay on an elongated *wurt* running parallel with the river. At the turn of the tenth century the *wurt* was extended northwards, and later to the south. A road paved with timbers crossed the *wurt*, with paths running east and west from it. In early medieval times a marshy area 100 m wide lay between the *wurt* and the Ems. Since this foreshore flooded at high tide and dried out at low tide, flat-bottomed vessels and early cogs could easily reach the place. At low water the ships were unloaded on to the dried-out marsh. In the eleventh century, when wharves became common, at which ships could moor afloat, the creek running east of the *wurt* was deepened. Larger cogs and carracks could now unload at the quays. At this time the *wurt* was densely built over with small houses built from wooden staves, resembling the early mercantile and craftsmen's settlements such as Hedeby. From the twelfth century the groups of buildings became larger. The town owed its development into the chief port and trading centre of the region to its continuing waterborne links to the Ems and the North Sea.

Trading towns built on long *wurten*

In its layout, the Emden of the early Middle Ages resembles other single-street villages built on elongated *wurten*, of the type that was common in the North Sea marshes between Groningen in north Holland and the Butjadingen peninsula at the mouth of the Weser, opposite modern Bremerhaven. In contrast to the round *wurten*, whose villages were chiefly engaged in farming, the long wurten were small settlements of traders and craftsmen. Having been enclosed by dykes, many of these *wurten* have retained their round or elongated form to this day. The long *wurten* were typically situated close to an estuary or bay with rivers or creeks connecting them with the interior. They thus had a protected position, and good facilities for mooring or beaching ships. The single street of houses ran directly along the river bank.

These townships were crossroads between sea routes and a densely populated, agricultural hinterland. Their economic importance lay in the organisation of short- and long-range trade. It was here that the indigenous products of the marshes were exchanged for goods imported from distant places by sea. Historical and archaeological sources indicate the existence of a landed upper class, who controlled output that exceeded their own needs, and organised its sale in export markets. Meat, wool, and skins, textiles, articles made from bone and antlers, as well as metal items, were among the goods offered by the landowners that were taken on board seagoing ships at the long *wurten*.

In later times many of these ports lost their role in long-haul trade, because the waterways silted up. Such was the fate of towns like Jemgum on the Ems, and Groothusen and Langwarden in eastern Friesland.

Dithmarschen

Heading further north, ships sailed along the marshy Dithmarschen coastline north of the Elbe estuary. Here there were no specialised trading *wurten*, but it is probable that vessels could follow creeks inland to a number of *wurt*-built villages.

In the early Middle Ages, Dithmarschen, lying between the Eider and Elbe estuaries, came into the purview of the Franks, seeking to extend their power northwards following the subjugation of the Saxons to Frankish rule. With its extensive marshes between isolated, sparsely settled, sandy uplands, the country remained difficult to control, with the exception of the high ridge near Albersdorf, and even that was not easily accessible. Hence, the maritime transport routes were all the more important.

North from the river Eider

The estuary of the Eider was an important maritime crossroads, since ships could sail further up the Eider, then up the river Treene as far as Hollingstedt, whence freight was transported 17 km over land to Hedeby on the Baltic side of Jutland. In this way North Sea and Baltic trade was connected across the narrowest point of the Jutland peninsula. As early as Roman times the inhabitants of the *wurten* around the Eider estuary profited from long-distance trade, and this was still the case in the early Middle Ages. On the *wurt* at Tofting, near modern Tönning, at the head of the Eider, imported Roman ceramics have been found: the prestigious *terra sigillata*. Articles found at the early medieval marshland settlement of Elisenhof include ceramics and combs from Friesland, whetstones and stirrups from Scandinavia, millstones of Rhenish basalt and decorative buckles from the Frankish empire.

Other ships sailed still further northward along the west coast of Jutland. However, it seems that the shipmasters were unwilling to negotiate this coast, with its offshore islands, narrow channels, shallows and tidal sea marshes. It was easier for the flat-bottomed boats of the early Middle Ages, since they could safely be grounded on a falling tide. From the High Middle Ages it became more difficult for the larger and deeper-draught cogs to find a course along this stretch of coast.

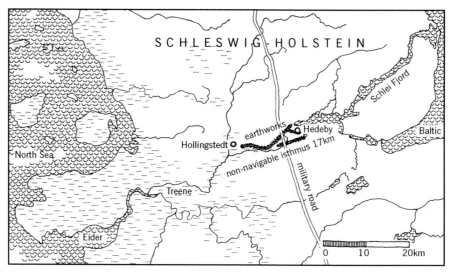

From the Eider estuary ships could sail upriver to Hollingstedt, from where goods were transported 17 km overland to Hedeby.

RIBE AND THE NORTH SEA COAST OF JUTLAND

In the early Middle Ages ships, leaving northern Friesland behind them, steered a course up the coast of Jutland, and reached the small estuary known as the Ribe Å (stream or creek). From there it was a further 5 km to the town of Ribe; this Viking settlement on the North Sea was the first one to be reached by Friesian sailors on their way northwards.

Like so many other trading posts, Ribe grew up at the intersection of land and sea routes. Around AD 700 there was a settlement on the bank of the Ribe Å, which soon developed into a small entrepôt and market. Merchants came here and set up their sales stalls, and workshops were established. The land was divided into plots separated by ditches. It is possible that the settlement was at first only occupied during the trading activities of the summer months. Manufacturing trades grew up quickly. Glass beads, jewellery and combs were produced. Farmers from the surrounding countryside drove their livestock to Ribe. The small port of call soon became the most important urban centre on the west coast of Jutland. The discovery of 300 *sceattas*, small silver coins, a number of which were struck in Ribe, points to a relatively sophisticated administration. It is probable that the settlement was under the control of the Danish king.

From the early eighth century Ribe became an important entrepôt between western Europe and Scandinavia. Glass drinking vessels and ceramics from the Rhineland provide evidence, for example, of the importation of wine. At the market merchants could purchase livestock. To the south of the commercial district, a settlement of large post-houses and smaller huts grew up on a sandy promontory lying between marshy lowlands. The boundary of the township was at first marked by a ditch, then replaced by a rampart in the tenth century. By the mid-ninth century Ribe was already so famous that it attracted missionaries such as St Ansgar. Further development proceeded apace: as early as 948 Ribe was nominated as a bishopric. It is possible that by this time the core of the settlement had moved to the south side of the river. Throughout the Middle Ages and beyond, Ribe was the most important religious and economic centre on the west coast of Jutland. This is not surprising, since north of Ribe there are no rivers or fjords of any size running into the interior, with the exception of Limfjord, which dissects the northern tip of Jutland.

From around AD 700, Ribe, near modern Esbjerg, developed into the most important trading centre on the west coast of Jutland.

ACROSS THE SKAGERRAK TO NORWAY

Vessels continuing northwards up the west coast of Jutland could either sail through the Limfjord to the Kattegat and thence into the Baltic, or else cross two dangerous stretches of sea, the Jammerbugt (Bay of Sorrows) on the north-western shore of Jutland, and the Skagerrak, beyond which lay Norway. Here, the shifting sandbanks and unpredictable currents were made more dangerous by violent storms, which could blow up near the coast. As recently as 1927 the *Handbuch der deutschen Marineleitung* (German Admiralty Handbook) issued a warning about this stretch of coast:

> *The northwest coast of Jutland is a dangerous coastline. On the stretch from Hangstholm to Skagen Point [the northern tip of Jutland] there are no harbours in which to seek shelter. The shore is completely exposed to the prevailing winds, which are usually stormy. The mighty Atlantic swell rolls unhindered on to the coast from the NW to NNW, between Scotland and Norway. The high surf that builds up on the rapidly shelving sea-bottom, has caused the loss of many ships and human lives. Sailors should therefore avoid this coast in all except offshore winds, and should regard lighthouses and beacons more as warnings than leading-lights.*

Kaupang

The crews of the little Viking ships must also have been glad when they had got across the Skagerrak and reached the fjord in southern Norway, at the head of which lay the port of Kaupang. At its seaward end the fjord was protected by numerous small islands. Kaupang was probably the same 'Sciringesheal' described by the Norwegian merchant, Ottar. The name Kaupang, which originally meant 'market', now survives only in a farm, on whose land lie a large number of Viking burial mounds. Today a meadow slopes gently down to the edge of the fjord. This means that in former times ships could easily be run up on the shore here. In the tidal range of the flat beach there was surfaced access to two 'ship landings', which are now permanently dry owing to a rise in the level of the land. One of these consisted of piles with bundles of brushwood laid on a stone foundation, and the other was a long gravel walkway. Both of these led up to a group of houses near the shore. In archaeological excavations of six of the buildings, clinker of iron and bronze was found, as well as smelting-pots and waste material from the manufacture of glass beads. Since no ovens or household refuse were found, these buildings were probably not occupied all year round. There was also evidence of a workshop for repairing ships.

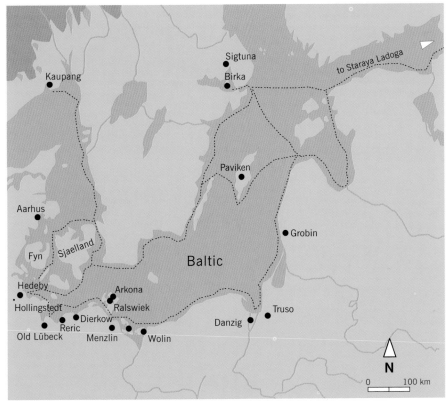

In the early Middle Ages a network of maritime trading towns (called *vik* in Norse) grew up around the Baltic. The northern Baltic was settled by Danish, Norwegian and Swedish Vikings, while Slavic tribes occupied the southern coast.

Archaeological finds also prove there was contact with the Rhineland, England and the Baltic. Soapstone and slate for whetstones reached Kaupang from the interior and were traded here for imported goods. The wreck of a Viking ship with a cargo of whetstone slate has been found some 15 km away on the coast near Kålsund. Since the township was not permanently inhabited, and had none of the fortifications customary in the troubled times of the tenth century, we may assume that Kaupang was abandoned at an earlier date. The reason for this may have been a change in sea level, but it could equally have been the result of the decline in Danish influence in southern Norway.

5 FROM HEDEBY TO VINETA:
EARLY TRADING POSTS ON THE BALTIC

From Kaupang the main sea route led into the Baltic region. We can tell from finds of coins that trade originating in the North Sea increasingly reached the Baltic from the eighth century onwards. In the seventh century, Merovingian coins (*trientes*) were still concentrated in the North Sea region, but *sceattas* dating from the eighth century have been found on the coasts of the Baltic.

THE BALTIC

Like the North Sea, the Baltic is a shallow sea, but has no large areas of coastal marshland. The tidal rise and fall is far less pronounced than in the North Sea. Nonetheless in the course of time the Baltic coastline underwent considerable natural transformation. An essential factor behind this was the fact that during the last Ice Age, the massive weight of the glaciers had pressed down on the land. Consequently, since the end of the Ice Age, the whole of Scandinavia has been gradually rising, with the result that the coastlines of Norway, Sweden and Finland have altered between the early Middle Ages and today. In some places archaeological finds have made it possible to reconstruct old coastlines. For example, the waterline at the end of the Ice Age, at its highest point today, is 286.5 m (nearly 1,000 ft) above sea level in north-central Sweden. It is chiefly in low-lying areas, such as those around Gulf of Bothnia in northern Sweden and western Finland, that the greatest horizontal shift in the coastline has taken place.

On the southern shore of the Baltic, by contrast, the waterline has changed far less, even though the land has been subject to movement. To balance the elevation of the Scandinavian land-mass, the level of the land around the southern Baltic has sunk. The fulcrum between the two geological processes, around which the tectonic plate has 'tipped', runs roughly NW–SE, from northern Jutland though the town of Anklam in Germany's Mecklenburg province, near to where the Polish frontier meets the Baltic. The types of coastline and shore in the southern Baltic differ greatly from those of Norway and Sweden. In places – for instance in Mecklenburg and West Pomerania – drowned coasts with hook-shaped sand bars have evolved. In the southern Baltic region the sea is bordered by the more or less steep-sided moraines left by the last Ice Age – chains of low hills formed from the deposits from melting glaciers. In places, estuaries, bays or large river deltas – such as those of the Oder and Vistula – cut deep into the interior. The coastline of eastern Denmark is similar in form to those of Mecklenburg and eastern Schleswig-Holstein. Here, access to the Baltic is barred by the large Danish islands of Fyn and Sjaelland, between which the Öresund and the straits known as the Great and Little Belt, provide a passage for shipping. Unlike the southern Baltic coast, the Scandinavian coastline is characterised by bays and skerries, and many rocky offshore islands. It was these natural phenomena that determined both the location of the early trading posts and the shipping routes.

EARLY MARITIME TRADING SITES

From the eighth century AD early entrepôts grew up at the intersection of land, river and sea transport routes; and from the ninth or tenth centuries these developed into large trading settlements. What characterised these townships was a combination of long-distance trade, artisanal activities and trades. At first it may have been groups of feudal landowners who wanted to profit from the commerce, until, from the ninth century, the ruling power of the day cast a covetous eye on these places. The feudal farmers owned their own landing stages. Initially, these agricultural communities no doubt did business on their own account until proto-urban structures developed. Small houses laid out in rows, and permanent harbour facilities formed the appropriate infrastructure for rapidly expanding long-distance trade. Even in the first phase of these trading posts, the farming communities produced articles from bone, horn and antlers. In addition precious and other metals were worked and iron utensils manufactured. These were used both in housebuilding and boatbuilding, Alongside their craft and trade output, the farmsteads supplied the necessary food from their livestock and cultivation.

These trading settlements were typified chiefly by the close economic links between hinterland and local markets, coastal trade and long-distance trade. The hinterland assured the subsistence of the inhabitants of the entrepôts. From here too came products like salt, amber, herring, iron bars and textiles, which were exported to distant markets. We can be sure that different regions were involved in this commerce. The western Baltic zone embraced Sweden, Gotland and Denmark, and extended as far as the North Sea area. Here the principal goods traded were iron bars and articles made from antler-horn. The iron ore came chiefly from southern Sweden. There were also containers made of Norwegian soapstone, and slate whetstones for sharpening knives, also from Norway. Another zone spread out from eastern Europe and extended along the great river systems to Byzantium.

Archaeology has revealed that more than 2,000 mainly Arabic silver coins from mints in the Middle East and Asia Minor, as well as Byzantine and Finno-Ugrian jewellery, reached the Baltic region in this way.

Merchants trading over long distances in their ships became intermediaries between the different cultures. As early as the eighth century Friesian merchants had reached the Baltic. Beside these, Danes, Swedes, Slavs and even Arabs were active as merchants. We have a clear picture of conditions in Wolin on the Polish river Dzwina. The eleventh-century historian, Adam of Bremen, tells us that foreign merchants from places including Saxony and the realm of Rus (these were Greeks), were quartered there. In other towns, like Arkona on the island of Rügen, foreign merchants are only mentioned as being short-term visitors. In times of danger, they sought refuge in the nearby tribal fortress, which is mentioned in connection with the Danish occupation in 1168. On the other hand, it was in the merchants' interest to avoid having maritime trading posts in the vicinity of military and political strongholds, in order to retain their independence. However, this independence was not absolute since it was paid for through levies.

Historical tradition often vaunts the wealth and size of these trading centres. The disadvantage of this 'propaganda' was that the entrepôts were subject to warlike attacks. Thus the official Frankish annals (*Annales regni Francorum*) for the year 808 tell us that the town of Reric, situated in *oceani litore* (meaning on the Baltic coast), in the land of the Slavic Obodrite tribe, was captured by the Danish king Gøttrik. Not satisfied with plundering the town, Gøttrik dragged the merchants off *ad portum, qui Sliesthorp dicitur*, the port named Sliesthorp, where he set them up in business again. This port was at the head of the Schlei fjord, and later became known as Hedeby, south of the modern town of Schleswig.

The merchants and their knowledge were clearly indispensable. Whereas they previously paid their dues to Slav princes, these now went into the pocket of the Danish king. The first written mention of two maritime trading posts in the south-western Baltic throws a brief ray of light on the economic structure of the coastal regions and gives us an idea of the importance of these ports.

HEDEBY

Travellers who, in the tenth century, sailed from the Baltic for some 35 km up the Schlei fjord, passed a landscape of raw, forest-covered moraines. The forest had only been cleared where there were rural settlements, such as that near Kosel. Shortly before the head of this arm of the sea, on the south shore, there was a protected bay, called the Hedeby Noor. It was here that one of the most important trading settlements in northern Europe grew up. At the time of its greatest expansion, Hedeby covered an area of some 25 hectares, surrounded by a semicircular rampart, and had a population of around 1,500. In the harbour, ships made fast to wooden jetties, which jutted out into the harbour basin. The Arab merchant Al-Tartoushi, who came to Hedeby from Tortosa in Spain in around AD 950, gives us an impression of the town:

> *[Hedeby] is a very large city at the further end of the world ocean.*
> *In its centre there are springs of fresh water. Its inhabitants are*
> *worshippers of Sirius, except for a small number who are Christians*
> *and have a church there... The town is poorly provided with land. The*
> *main source of food for the population is fish, since they are very*
> *numerous there. If children are born to one of the inhabitants, he*
> *throws them into the sea, in order to save himself the expense...*

More comprehensive than such fanciful accounts are the extensive archaeological investigations into the development and economic structure of Hedeby. For example, a settlement first grew up south of where the semicircular rampart was later built. In the ninth century – roughly at the time when the merchants from Reric were resettled there by Gøttrik – the population-centre shifted further north to the banks of a small brook running into the Noor. In the tenth century the stream was canalised and covered over with planks. While people washed their hands in the brook and doubtless tipped refuse into it, there were springs to provide fresh water. In the ninth or tenth centuries the centre of the town was criss-crossed with streets surfaced with baulks of timber. On both sides of the streets there were small, fenced areas on which stood dwellings, workshops and warehouses. The dwellings were usually rectangular buildings with two or three rooms. Excavations, geophysical investigations and underwater research in the harbour fill out the detail of our picture of this international trading centre. We know there were jetties built close

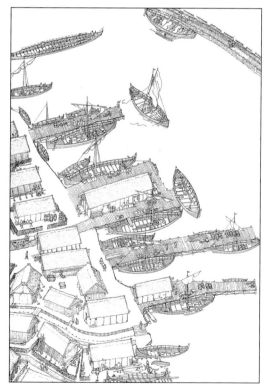

This reconstruction shows how the port of Hedeby, with its jetties and ships, might have looked in the tenth century.

to each other, protected by two palisades in the water with a wide gap between them. The construction of the jetties took place in several phases, beginning in 863; the latest one dates from 966. The older jetties in the central harbour area were orientated east–west and connected on the landward side to the ninth-century street system. Clearly of more recent date than the jetties was the wreck of a Viking ship (wreck 1), lying just offshore in shallow water.

From the mid-tenth century the early town was protected on the landward side by a 1,300 m-long semicircular rampart made of sods of turf, which still stands 10 m high today. On the south side, the rampart was extended into the water by the bow-shaped palisade already mentioned. In that period, it is probable that the central harbour area was abandoned, possibly as a result of increasing silting-up, and replaced by areas further along the shore. To the north of the rampart was a fortified position, a kind of 'stronghold'. However, it was not enough to prevent the trading post from being destroyed on several occasions. The saga of the Norwegian king Harald Hardrada (written by Snorri Sturluson, 1179–1241) tells how, in the course of his battles against the Danish king, Sven Estridsen, in 1050, Harald arrived with an army outside Hedeby and burned the town to the ground:

> *All Heidaby is burned down!*
> *Strangers will ask where stood the town.*
> *In our wild humour up it blazed,*
> *And Svein looks round him all amazed.*
> *All Heidaby is burned down!*
> *From a far corner of the town*
> *I saw, before the peep of morning,*
> *Roofs, walls, and all in flame high burning.*[1]

Sixteen years later we read in Adam of Bremen about the plundering of Hedeby by Slavs.

Thus the end of the extensive settlement within the ramparts of Hedeby came between 1050 and 1066 or 1070, if we accept the latest dendro-chronological dating. During this period there began the resettlement of the last inhabitants on the Old Town Hill in Schleswig, north of the Schlei. For a very brief period at most, the two settlements existed side by side. However, it was not the hostile assaults that led to the re-establishment of the town that is today's Schleswig (Danish *Slesvik*), but rather the shifts in political power

---

1 *Heimskringla* from the website of the Gutenberg Project (www.gutenberg.org/etext/598)

and developments in transport and commerce. In the new centre a royal court and a cathedral were soon founded. But there was another, decisive advantage offered by the town: in the High Middle Ages the deeper fairway allowed the transport of freight in cogs with a deeper draught, which would probably have had difficulty in entering Hedeby creek.

However, Schleswig, like Hedeby, was dependent not only on long-haul trade but also on the supply of food from the surrounding countryside. Hedeby was set amid agricultural land, linked to the town by merchants. Rural settlements – such as Kosel – delivered farm produce in exchange for combs and jewellery that were manufactured in Hedeby. In addition to this local commerce, long-distance trade was the distinguishing feature of this early medieval town. For Hedeby and Schleswig lay at the profitable intersection of various transport routes. West of the town ran the north–south road into Jutland, the Oxen Way. And from the North Sea ships could come up the rivers Eider and Treene as far as Holligstedt, where the cargoes – such as Carolingian drinking-vessels and millstones from Mayen basalt – were transferred to wagons and carried some 17 km east to Hedeby. There is as yet no evidence of ships landing at Hollingstedt in the early Middle Ages, though there have been archaeological finds there from that period. Luxury goods such as silver and silk reached Hedeby from the east, on ships plying the Baltic, and were exchanged there for wares from western Europe.

FROM HEDEBY INTO THE LAND OF THE SVEAS: THE VOYAGE OF ST ANSGAR TO BIRKA

Setting out from Hedeby, ships laden with fresh cargoes sailed down the Schlei into the Baltic, where they could head north to Sweden or Norway, or southwards along the coasts of lands settled by Slavs. One of these voyagers who, rather than trading, wanted to spread Christianity in the land of the Sveas – Sweden – was the Frankish monk Ansgar. In AD 829 he set out to sail to Birka, near modern Stockholm, in Sweden. The voyage was full of dangers. Once, the ship he was aboard was attacked by pirates, who robbed him of his valuable books and religious objects. They forced the holy man and his companions to abandon the ship. Nonetheless – as Ansgar's biographer, Rimbert, tells us – they reached Birka, where they were received by King Björn, and by the king's representative in the town, Herigar. The latter received baptism and Ansgar returned home. In about 850 Ansgar sailed once more to Birka, where he had been given permission to build a church. At that time Birka was already a thriving community. In this period, over a thousand years ago, the Mälar was not a landlocked lake as it is today, but an arm of the Baltic stretching far inland. By sailing up a narrow channel near the present town of Södertälje, seagoing ships could reach the trading port. However, they first had to be hauled across a narrow strip of land, and a special track was laid for this purpose.

From there they proceeded to Birka, situated on the island of Björkö. A settlement had grown up here as early as the eighth century, which subsequently increased in importance. By the tenth century we can assume that many small wooden houses huddled within the semicircular defensive rampart, which enclosed an area of 7 hectares. Access to the town of some 900 inhabitants was controlled on the south side by a stronghold, in which the townsfolk could take shelter in times of danger. The harbour was probably fortified as well. The population buried their dead in cemeteries to the east and south of the town. It is chiefly the finds from these graves that shed light on Birka's maritime trading links. Ships from Birka sailed to Hedeby, to the southern Baltic coast and far along the rivers of Russia.

Birka's existence depended on its accessibility to shipping. This was less favourable than in Hedeby's case, because of the barrier at the seaward exit of the Mälar. Since the land was gradually rising, it became more and more difficult to haul ships across the isthmus. For this reason shipping increasingly used the northern entrance to the Mälar, on which Stockholm stands today. But here the ships had to follow a winding course, sailing or rowing between countless skerries and islands. Taking this route, ships could more quickly reach the mouth of the river Fyriså, where the new port of Sigtuna lay. Unlike Birka, this town was situated at the heart of an emerging empire and was thus better suited as a centre of royal power than was an isolated town in the middle of a lake. Because of these political and geographical changes, Birka rapidly lost its importance after AD 1000.

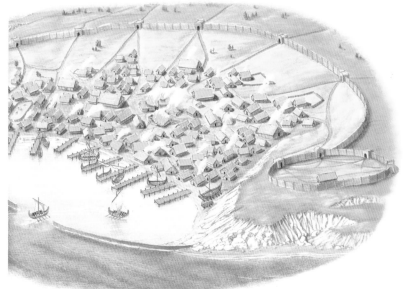

The trading centre of Birka in Sweden was situated on the island of Björkö in Lake Mälar, west of Stockholm.

THE SOUTHERN BALTIC COAST

Like the Danes and Swedes, the Slav tribes on the southern coast of the Baltic participated in seaborne trade. These tribes included the Ranians, the Obodrites, the Pomeranians and probably also the Luticians. But trade was always accompanied by piracy; the Ranians, who lived on the island of Rügen, were notorious for piracy. The extent of long-distance seaborne trade and the speed of its development followed the western example and rapidly encompassed the western and eastern Baltic – in other words a region that, like Scandinavia, had never formed part of the Roman empire.

As a consequence of Charlemagne's war against the Saxons, the area of Obodrite settlement had already, by the end of the eighth century, come into direct contact with the Danes, the dominant power in the Baltic. This encounter also encouraged the efforts of the Slavic tribes to combine into larger groups. Furthermore, the contact with Danes and Franks brought about economic and social changes.

The western Slavs – the Vagrians in eastern Holstein, as well as the Obodrites, Wilzi and Rugians in Mecklenburg and Western Pomerania – now established a series of Baltic trading posts as part of the network of sea routes that was steadily gaining in importance. Inland, too, changes came about. For example, in eastern Holstein many small fortified Slavic villages gave way to larger units, in the process of which Starigard (now Oldenburg) and Old Lübeck gained in importance as centres of aristocratic power, The Holstein town of Oldenburg was formerly a port on a bay of the Baltic before access to the sea gradually silted up and the entrance became ever more difficult for shipping. Old Lübeck was more favourably situated on the sea and did not suffer from the same limitations, which was why it became the seat of the Obodrite princes.

Old Lübeck

The fortress of Old Lübeck, enclosed by an earth rampart, was built in the ninth century on a peninsula between the rivers Trave and Schartau, in south-eastern Holstein. In the eleventh century it was the permanent seat of the Obodrite princes Gottschalk and Heinrich, and attracted trade with its accessibility to shipping. Two settlements grew up outside the walls, one to the south and the other to the west, in which artisan trades and local as well as long-distance commerce were concentrated. The southern settlement consisted of small rectangular houses, most of which were built in blocks, along which ran surfaced streets. Wicker fences separated the individual areas from each other. To provide a better berth for ships, the low bank of the Trave was reinforced. In the course of hostilities between Slavs, Saxons and Danes, the castle was destroyed. After this, the conquest of eastern Holstein by the

Germans in 1138 created new political and economic conditions, and with the riverside market a new long-distance trading centre grew up on Lübeck's Old Town Hill, which had already been inhabited in Slavic times.

Reric/Gross-Strömkendorf

As southern neighbours of the Danes, and eastern neighbours of the Saxons, the Obodrites were already important allies of the Franks and hence appear frequently in the annals of the Frankish empire. As already mentioned, the imperial annals also describe how, in 808, a trading post on the Mecklenburg coast, under Obodrite rule, was destroyed by the Danish king, Gøttrik. The Danes called this town Reric. We know little more about this event, except that it was certainly a seaborne attack. At the time of the attack, the inhabitants of Reric owed allegiance to the Obodrite prince Dražko, whose seat was the castle of Mecklenburg. The Franks could not have been happy about this assault, since Reric was one of the nearest harbours on the Baltic, whose development was very much in the interest of the Frankish monarchs. But where exactly was this southern Baltic trading settlement located?

Archaeological investigations in the 1990s led to the discovery of a mass of finds in Gross-Strömkendorf on the Bay of Wismar, which is probably the Reric mentioned in the imperial Frankish annals. A centre of long-distance trade was partially excavated and near it, to the east, were two fortresses. Evidence from the archaeological finds and tree-ring dating tells us that these fortifications existed at the same time as the commercial port. The fact that in this region the politico-military power-centres lay at some distance from the seaports, is proved by archaeological research. Still further inland stood the Mecklenburg, one of the chief strongholds of the Slavic Obodrites. Reric thus formed part of the Mecklenburgers' fortified area, a *civitas*, as Adam of Bremen, writing about 1070, called such areas. To judge from archaeological research into the settlement, this area extended for more than 20 km, between the Bay of Wismar and Lake Schwerin.

Another reason why it is so difficult to identify Reric is because the coastal landscape has changed a good deal over the past thousand years. Thus the location today of archaeological finds from the onetime trading centre is at a point where the sea has since broken through. This position is very unusual, since the known trading settlements of Rostock/Dierkow, Ralswiek, Menzlin and Wolin all lay more than 10 km from the sea on riverbanks or inlets of the Baltic, in order to be safe from storm-surges and sudden attacks by pirates. The same is true of nearly all the comparable sites in Scandinavia, such as Ribe or Hedeby, both located at the head of an arm of the sea.

However, because of the considerable erosion of the coastline, several areas settled in the Slav period today lie beneath the sea. It is possible that a thousand years ago the Bay of Wismar was dotted with numerous small islands, the remains of which can still be identified in Walfisch ('Whale') Island and many sandbanks just below the surface. These islands broke the force of the Baltic surf and the creeks running between them provided navigable routes for shipping. A creek between the island of Poel and the mainland north of Wismar, which is over 5 m deep today, was probably the only navigable approach to the trading post in the Slavic period. Taking this topography into account, we can see that Reric would indeed have been in a typically protected position comparable with the other maritime trading-posts of the time.

Archaeological measurements lead to the conclusion that the Reric settlement covered an area of 17 hectares. Remains of oak posts near the present shore of the Baltic suggest the presence of a harbour or reinforcement of the bank. Archaeology also shows that the site of finds near Gross-Strömkendorf existed as a settlement of merchants and craftsmen in the eighth and early ninth centuries and maintained close relations with the Frankish empire. Hence, it is quite possible that Gross-Strömkendorf was the same Reric that was seized by Gøttrik in AD 808. At all events, Gøttrik's seamen must have known or reconnoitred the tricky waters between the islands, with their hidden navigable passages.

Sadly, the excavations themselves have so far yielded little solid evidence of the settlement structure of this trading port. However, what have been found are rows of cellar-like buildings dug into the ground, in which craftsmen had their workshops. The town's dead were usually cremated, and their ashes and bones buried in a nearby cemetery. In addition to the 44 cremation-graves, 16 body-graves have also been discovered. Of particular significance are three graves, in which the position of rivets makes it clear that these were boat-graves. The custom of burying their dead in boats, as evidenced by the iron rivets that were found, makes it clear that these were burials in the Scandinavian tradition. These burial customs thus indicate intensive contacts across the Baltic. Like the boat-shaped arrangements of stones in Menzlin, near Anklam on the Stettiner Haff (which today straddles the German–Polish border), and the ship-grave at Ralswiek on the island of Rügen, they show how the sea created cultural links.

Dierkow and Menzlin: trading ports of the Wilzi

We can assume that there were also maritime trading posts at the mouth of the river Warnow near Rostock, since the lower reaches of the Warnow provided the Slavic Wilzi tribe with a gateway to the Baltic. Hence it is no surprise that in the area round Rostock several caches of treasure from the ninth and tenth centuries have been unearthed. The trading ports that grew up need not always have been very large – groups of farmers, who wanted to profit from foreign trade founded smaller entrepôts, such as Dierkow near Rostock, on the eastern bank of the Warnow. In this settlement, which flourished in the eighth and ninth centuries, not only have Slavic artefacts come to light, but also the remains of drinking-vessels from the Rhineland in the form of so-called 'Tating' jugs and brooches from Gotland. Historical records from the eleventh and twelfth centuries indirectly stress the importance of this estuary, since they mention several castles. The extent to which this strategic stretch of coastline was fought over is shown by the Saxon campaign of conquest in 1121, which destroyed the castle of the Kessinian prince Zuentibaldi.

Just as the Warnow was the Baltic gateway for the Kessinians, a branch of the Wilzi tribe, the river Peene gave the eastern territory of the Wilzi access to the sea. Conversely, goods arriving by sea could be transported up the rivers to the interior. Hence a trading port grew up in the ninth century near Menzlin on the Peene. In the eleventh century Adam of Bremen called this place the 'sea port' for shipping in the area of the Oder estuary. In the hinterland behind Menzlin there was an important Wilzi fortress, which was probably the same one as that recorded as early as AD 789 as the stronghold of the Wilzi king Dragowit (*civitas Dragowiti*). It is likely that the fortress stood near the present Tollensee lake.

Rügen

For the chroniclers of the Frankish and Ottonian empires, living far from the sea, the island of Rügen, some way offshore in the Baltic, must have seemed very remote in comparison to the territories of the Obodrites and Wilzi. For sailors, on the other hand, Rügen was an important landfall, on which the light of recorded history was shed as early as AD 700, when the island attracted the attention of Anglo-Saxon missionaries for the first time. So it was that ships brought not only goods but also new ideas and religious concepts from over the sea. Archaeologists have revealed two trading settlements on Rügen, at Ralswiek and Arkona. While Ralswiek was purely dedicated to trade, Arkona, on the northern point of the island, formed the fortified centre of a *provincia*. The harbour and settlement of Arkona were situated near the castle. In Ralswiek, graves were found containing the remains of wagons. This indicates a Scandinavian burial custom, as were the boat-shaped stone arrangements in the grave-field at Menzlin, near the Peene.

Burial-places marked by lines of stones in the shape of a ship can be found on the German island of Rügen in the Baltic, as well as in Sweden.

Wolin–Vineta

If sailors continued on a south-easterly course from Arkona, skirting the island of Usedom, they would have reached Wolin on the island of the same name (now in Polish territory, some 40 km north of Szczecin [Stettin]). Sailing up the estuary of the Dzwina, ships would reach one of the largest of the early trading settlements on the Baltic. The town lay on the east bank of the Dzwina on the island of Wolin. The Dzwina provided a navigable route across the open waters of the Stettiner Haff to the river Peene and the landward shore of Usedom island in the west, and more importantly to the river Oder in the south, where ships could reach Stettin. These important waterways intersected here with an overland trade route, which ran from the Elbe along the southern Baltic coast through Menzlin and Laage.

Writing in the early eleventh century, Adam of Bremen called the section running through Mecklenburg the *via regia*, or King's Road, and that in Pomerania the *via antiqua*, or Old Road. The chronicler goes on to note that the overland journey from Hamburg to Wolin took seven days, but that it was also possible to reach Wolin by sea from Hedeby or Oldenburg. The direct onward voyage from Wolin to Novgorod by ship took fourteen days. The town of Wolin was founded in the eighth or ninth century, at the point where the *via antiqua* crossed the river Dzwina. It was it its most prosperous in the second half of the eleventh century and was then abandoned.

The fame of this Slavic town spread far and wide: the Spanish Jew, Ibrahim Ibn Jakub, who travelled with Arab envoys to visit the German emperor Otto I, wrote that 'they [the people of Wolin] possess a mighty city on the ocean, which has twelve gates. It also has wharves made from tree-trunks split in half.'

The seaward approach to the estuary was made easier by a beacon, probably the kind of fire visible for many miles that was copied from the Byzantines, and which Adam of Bremen describes as *olla Vulcani*, or Vulcan's Pot. He talks of 'Greek fire', a particular Byzantine invention, which could not be extinguished by water.

Adam gives a picturesque description of Wolin itself in the second book of his history of the Church:

> *It is the greatest city in Europe. There dwell Slavs together with*
> *members of other peoples, with Greeks and barbarians. But*
> *immigrants from Saxony are also granted the right to dwell there,*
> *provided they do not flaunt the symbols of their Christianity.*

Even more imaginative is the description by Helmold of Bosau in his 'Chronicle of the Slavs', written in 1170. In a chapter entitled *De civitate Vineta*, he already talks of the city in the past tense. He refers to the period up to the middle of the eleventh century, before its destruction. In his mind, too, the city to which he, for the first time, gives the name *Vineta*, is the greatest city of the Slavs. In his own work, Helmold made very free use of the chronicle of Adam of Bremen, and added a moralistic note to his account. These two accounts were enlarged upon in an even more picturesque way by the monk Angelus of Stargard in 1345. So was born the legend of a fabled city called Vineta, submerged under the Baltic like an eastern Atlantis. Archaeological excavations show us how we should really visualise the Wolin of the early Middle Ages.

Sailors crossing the Baltic and arriving in the mouth of the Dzwina would have seen a settlement stretching along a gentle slope down to the river. From the mid-ninth century, after an earlier settlement had been destroyed, the new town centre was surrounded by a rampart up to 8 m in height, beyond which ran a ditch. Additional protection was afforded by a belt of marshy land. Adjoining the fortified centre were two further areas of population to the north and south. A street ran north and south through the core of the town, with a gate at either end. Farther from the town, beyond the suburbs, were several more settlements on both sides of the river Dzwina. These supplied the early town with fish and farm produce, and with pottery and other artefacts and services. Our picture of the settlement is completed by cemeteries such as that on 'Gallows Hill' north of the early town, and the main cemetery on 'Windmill Hill', which revealed 5,000 to 8,000 cremations and body-burials.

Ships arriving here from the north first came to the jetty in the northern suburb where a settlement of merchants and craftsmen stood on 'Silver Hill', protected by a rampart from the ninth or tenth centuries onwards. At the highest point on Silver Hill was the market square, mentioned as *forum et taberna* (marketplace and inn) in historical sources around 1140. Around the square the land was sparsely built over with houses dug into the ground. An upturned boat served as a roof for a workshop. Numerous fireplaces are evidence of blacksmiths, foundries and workshops making jewellery and artefacts from antlers. There were smokeries for fish. Finds of boat-rivets also indicate that ships were built and repaired there.

Further to the south, adjoining 'Silver Hill', was the actual town centre protected by a rampart. From the ninth to the twelfth centuries, the harbour quarter with its quays consisted of densely packed areas of small houses built from earth blocks or wicker walls. The plots were clearly marked out and separated by a grid of streets running parallel with and down to the river.

Excavations reveal the development of Wolin's port, which figured so largely in foreign trade from the ninth to the twelfth centuries. Initially the ships were probably beached, before a wooden quay was built. The piling of the quay on the Dzwina consisted of oak trunks split in half, just as Ibn Jakub described. The outer side was reinforced by horizontal beams, while the landward side was firmly anchored in the ground. This technical solution is known from other Slavic structures of the ninth and tenth centuries, for instance the temple in Gross-Raden, in Mecklenburg. Because of the boggy subsoil, bunches of brushwood and oak timbers were laid down, before the walls leading down to the riverbank could be built, and the space between them filled in with earth, then given a deck of tree trunks. However, nothing could prevent the wharves from subsiding from the effects of water and frost. What is more, the sea level in the Baltic rose. The normal level of the river Oder is today about 160 cm (5 ft 3 ins) higher than it was in Slavic times. For this reason, around 955 AD a new quay had to be constructed. In addition, around the turn of the tenth and eleventh centuries, jetties were built into the river. The need for these jetties may have been the growing size of the ships. If the waterfront ran the full length of the town centre that was protected by ramparts, it must have been 250 m to 300 m long. This would make Wolin the largest port in the Baltic. The waterfront included a shipyard, as is shown by the finds of rivets, boat components and a stem-post.

The river Dzwina was crossed by a bridge, written evidence of which admittedly only goes back to 1124, but which may well have existed in the ninth or tenth centuries. The overall settlement extended for a length of 4 km along the west bank of the Dzwina and probably numbered 6,000 to 8,000 inhabitants. True, Ibn Jakub had not seen Wolin himself, but the statements he passes on about the size of the town are unlikely to be an exaggeration. According to Adam of Bremen, a wide variety of peoples – 'barbarians, Greeks and Saxons' – gathered here. But when he writes of 'Greeks', he is probably thinking of Russians or Byzantines, since they all belonged to the Orthodox Church. And the term 'barbarian' is probably applied to all the Baltic races. In the port of Wolin there probably also lived a Norwegian merchant, who may have stored his goods here in winter, in order to have them ready for the next sailing season. However, this man has left us nothing more than a small wooden stick decorated with runes. The numerous combs of the Friesian type found in the southern district leads us to think there may have been a Friesian community there.

Until the mission to Pomerania by Otto of Bamberg, those permanent inhabitants, and incomers who were not Christian, worshipped a variety of gods. Evidence of this is the ninth-century temple uncovered in the southern part of the town, which was probably dedicated to a local deity, and which visitors would notice at the highest point of the town. In the tenth century, the original building was replaced by a more impressive new structure. In the area around the temple many small idols and amulets have been found. It is likely that inside the temple there stood quite a large statue, perhaps of the four-faced Svantevit, which was still there for Otto of Bamberg to see. Sources from the era of the Christian missionaries also mention a sacred spear stuck into a post, apparently as a display.

The archaeological finds enable us to distinguish the individual districts of the town of Wolin. Thus, in the south-eastern quarter as well as in the southern suburb beyond the walls, and on Silver Hill, there were numerous craftsmen's workshops. Near the harbour, the main activity was the fashioning of amber, a highly popular commodity for trading. Near the town centre there was a concentration of workers in antler-horn. Here combs were manufactured, which resemble the Friesian and Scandinavian designs. Bronze was also worked, and a large number of potters produced ceramic ware for domestic use. Finds of imported goods underline the extensive trading contacts between the Oder estuary and Scandinavia. Not only were salt, fish, leather and skins traded, but also iron and corn.

All the emerging early towns around the Oder estuary had the advantage of a fertile and productive hinterland. Wolin thus became caught up in the regional power-struggle between Danes and the emergent centralised power of Poland. As Ibn Jakub tells us, war broke out in 963 between the people of Wolin and Duke Mieszko I of Poland After the defeat of Wolin it became the most important port in the Polish realm of the Piast dynasty. In this period the town experienced a revival of its fortunes until, from the mid-eleventh century onwards, dynastic quarrels among the Polish nobility and military campaigns by the Danes led to the final disappearance of the town. As early as 1098 we hear of a Danish attack on Wolin, which the Danes called Jomsburg. Many caches of treasure unearthed in the vicinity of the town point indirectly to these troubled times. Then, finally, in the campaigns of 1173 and 1174, Wolin was destroyed by the Danish king Valdemar, who had focused his ambitions on the region of the Oder estuary. Before the town was burned to the ground, it was abandoned in 1176 by its inhabitants, who then settled in nearby Kamin. Sources in the high and late Middle Ages describe local trading activity in Wolin, but to this day the town has never regained its erstwhile position as the commercial metropolis of the Baltic.

The Baltic coast

A ship that sailed from where the castle of Szczecin (Stettin) stands today, downstream past Wolin, could follow the navigable route from the mouth of the Dzwina north-westwards along the Pomeranian coast to the island of Rügen, or eastward to the mouth of the Vistula. Between the Oder and the Vistula, the vessel would pass Kołobrzeg (Kolberg) and Puck, before reaching the mighty walls of Gdańsk (Danzig). On the eastern side of the Vistula estuary lay another trading centre, named Truso, which is known from written sources of the ninth century. From there the sea route followed the coasts of Lithuania, Latvia and Estonia, as far as Rus, the early Russian state ruled from Kiev.

6 FROM THE VARANGIANS TO THE GREEKS: ALONG THE RUSSIAN RIVERS

INTO THE LAND OF RUS

The long voyages from the Baltic, along the Russian river systems to Byzantium (Constantinople), are among the most fascinating chapters in maritime cultural history. In the early Middle Ages the crossroads of this route was the Swedish island of Gotland. The landowning farmers of the island were responsible for a large part of the maritime trade between Scandinavia and Russia and thus became intermediaries between east and west. In order to assess Gotland's trading links it is important to know that there was only one passage from the Swedish mainland to the island in which the seafarer could keep land in sight for the whole voyage. This route lay from the northern tip of the island of Öland eastwards to the small island of Karlsö, off Gotland's south-west coast. At the highest point of the island a stone cairn had been built as a navigation-mark. Beyond this the bay of Norderhamn provided a sheltered landfall for medieval shipping. From the mid-seventh century onwards ships sailed further east to Grobin near modern Liepaja in Latvia. Even before the Viking age, this passage was made across open sea.

It was Swedish Vikings who made their way up the Gulf of Finland and into the lands of the Russian Slavs. Their ships sailed as far as the mouth of the Neva, on which St Petersburg now stands, and which flows out from an inland sea, Lake Ladoga. From the southern shore of the lake, a watercourse took them along the Volkhov and the Lovat–Dnieper river system into the lands of Rus, then on across the Black Sea to Byzantium. The voyage from Wolin to Novgorod on the Volkhov, north of Lake Ilmen, took about two weeks.

THE VARANGIANS

Swedish merchants, who penetrated the vast expanses of Russia, became the instruments of cultural exchange. The question of how great was the influence of the Vikings on the shaping of the early Russian state and its cities is no less disputed than the names 'Varangian' and 'Rus' themselves. The words *Varyag* in Russian, and the Greek *Varangoi* in Byzantine sources were both derived from an Old Icelandic term meaning 'members of a sworn brotherhood'. The word *Rus* has its roots in the Balto-Finnish term *Ruotsi*, meaning Sweden, but could also be derived from the Swedish *ródr*, meaning a 'crew of oarsmen'. It was, of course, on ships that could be sailed or rowed that the Swedish Vikings reached Russia.

So it was that, in ancient Russia, Scandinavian merchants were simply known as Varangians, but confusingly the same term was applied to other groups, Russians among them, including mercenaries, military leaders, refugees, privileged visitors, merchants, Christian martyrs, royal guests, governors or administrators. In the eleventh and twelfth centuries 'Varangians' often crop up as bodyguards to Russian princes. Thus, in Russia at that time, there were many people referred to as 'Varangians'.

The Arab Ibn Fadlan is the first writer to record his impressions of a group of Scandinavian merchants, whom he met on the Volga in the year 922.

> *I saw the Rus, when they arrived on their trading trips and stopped on the Volga. I have never seen more perfect physical specimens, as tall as date-palms, fair-haired and with a rosy complexion; they wear neither tunics nor caftans, but the men wear a garment that covers one side of their body and leaves one hand free. All the men have an axe, a sword and a knife, which they carry with them at all times... Every woman wears her garment over both breasts, and carries a small chest made of iron, silver, copper or gold... each chest has a ring, from which a knife hangs. The women wear neck-bands of gold and silver... their most treasured items of jewellery are green glass beads.*

The Scandinavians initially arrived as merchants along the river route to the Russian interior. They especially coveted the valuable furs, which were sold at top prices and exchanged for swords and other arms, as well as for jewellery and amber, and even slaves. Goods that came up from the Lower Volga included Arabian silver coins, beads from rock crystal and cornelian, cowrie shells, small glass oil-lamps, harnesses and saddles, as well as textiles and spices. The purchase, transport and resale of valuable merchandise carried high risks. No wonder the merchants demanded and achieved high profit margins.

STARAYA LADOGA AND THE LAKE LADOGA REGION

The first trading post the merchants reached on this long voyage was situated on the shores of Lake Ladoga. The port of Staraya Ladoga (Old Ladoga), called *Adeigjuborg* by the Vikings, was one of the oldest trading centres in eastern Europe, situated where the river Volkhov flows northward into Lake Ladoga. At the intersection of trade routes from the Baltic and from the south, a market grew up here in the eighth century and became the most important in northern Russia in the ninth and tenth centuries. We may assume that Staraya Ladoga was not a city in the proper sense, but probably a trading post where a large number of craftsmen had taken up residence.

The place acted as a magnet for regional trade among the indigenous population and the Finns who inhabited the south-eastern shores of Lake Ladoga. These Finns exchanged furs for jewellery, weapons, textiles and crockery. Thus there rapidly grew up workshops, inns for foreign merchants and blocks of dwellings. Ibn Fadlan describes how houses built in a similar fashion to those of the Lower Volga provided accommodation for merchants. After the native people had been converted to Christianity, no fewer than eight churches and monasteries were built here. As well as Finns and Scandinavians, there were also Slavs living in Ladoga, and indeed a council of the Slav and Finnish tribes would meet here. If we are to believe the Nestor Chronicle from around 1113, this council summoned three brothers from Scandinavia to pacify and control the region. One of them, named Rorik (*Ryurik* in Russian) was soon to subject the whole of northern and upper Rus to his rule. Thus Ladoga became the seat of a novel kind of alliance. When the capital was moved to Novgorod, and then to Kiev, Ladoga remained a self-governing region under Rorik's successors. The predominant influence in the city was in the hands of merchants, artisans, princely administrators and warriors.

FROM THE VARANGIANS TO THE GREEKS

The principal route, which was given the name 'From the Varangians to the Greeks', ran from the Baltic, along the Gulf of Finland, parallel to the Russian coast, and then along the river Neva and across the lake to Staraya Ladoga. This was the first port of call on the journey. From the southern shore of Lake Ladoga, ships then followed the river Volkhov upstream to Novgorod. In the lower reaches, the ships would pass numerous Slavic settlements, until they reached the point where the river enters Lake Ilmen. Close by stood the island fortress of Holmgardir, another market centre that thrived in the ninth and tenth centuries and was populated both by Scandinavians and Slavs. Situated at the intersection of these river routes, the whole area of lakes and islands, the 'Gates of Novgorod', became the centre of a state that developed in northern Rus. In the centre of Novgorod stood its citadel or kremlin (*kreml* in Russian), which in the tenth century was enclosed by an earthen rampart. Even today the city is still dominated by the golden domes and spires of St Sophia's cathedral, built in the eleventh century. Major excavations in the medieval city have revealed a stratification up to 6 m deep, containing numerous dwelling-houses, workshops, streets and archaeological finds.

On the eastern shore of Lake Ilmen ships could enter the river Msta and follow it as far as it was navigable. Then after an overland stretch, merchants could sail down the Volga to the Caspian Sea. Another possibility was to cross the lake to its south side and follow the course of the Lovat. However, freight would have to be transported for quite a long distance to the western Dvina and thence be hauled overland again to reach the Dnieper.

Ships sailing southward down the Dnieper would first pass Gnezdovo, near modern Smolensk, where there was a colony that may have been exclusively Scandinavian, but more probably comprised various races. Here, ships could, if necessary, be repaired and refitted. After this the merchants would pass a number of riverside fortresses before reaching Kiev and finally the Black Sea. Thus the Dnieper provided the fastest link between the realm of Kiev and Byzantium. Downstream from Kiev the main axis of this route 'from the Varangians to the Greeks' was also known as the 'Greek Way'. When the river froze in winter, goods could still be transported on sledges.

Kiev, on the banks of the Dnieper, in what is now the Ukraine, and then known to the Vikings as *Kœnugardr*, was another important early urban settlement. Like Novgorod, Kiev was also ruled by Scandinavians in the tenth century. Not until the following century do we first hear of rulers with Slavic names. From that time onwards, the name 'Rus' was given to the evolving Russian state. In the High Middle Ages Kiev replaced Novgorod as the capital of Rus. Regardless of Scandinavian influence the routes formed by lakes and rivers were the essential foundation for this process.

Excavations in Kiev have given impressive confirmation of written accounts of the early development of the city. The original township on the Dnieper was built on and around three hills. In the ninth century – before the advent of the Northmen – a large wooden temple was built on one of the hills. And in the late ninth and tenth centuries merchants and artisans settled at the foot of this hill. In the period that followed, the town rapidly increased in size, and thanks to outer fortifications and a *kreml* it now became a redoubtable citadel. Excavations have revealed administrative buildings, places of worship and dwellings.

From Kiev, shipping continued down the Dnieper. Once the vessels had negotiated the dangerous rapids above the estuary, described in Chapter 1, merchants crossed the Black Sea to Byzantium. The capital of the Greek-speaking empire had been renamed Constantinople by the Roman emperor Constantine in the fourth century AD. When the Norsemen beheld the

Novgorod, situated where the river Volkhov flows into Lake Ilmen, was strongly fortified in the tenth century.

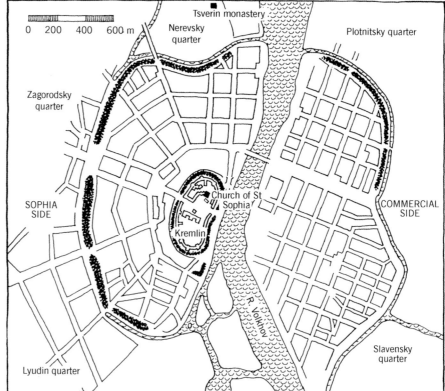

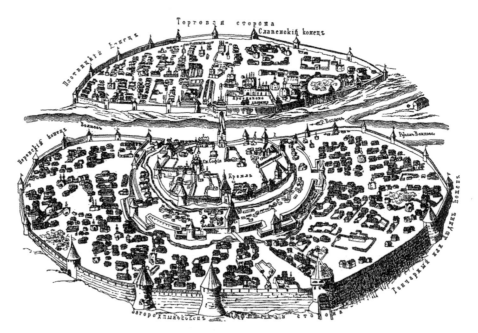

In this sixteenth-century depiction of Novgorod, the walled Kremlin can be recognised in the centre of the city.

greatest city they had ever seen, they called it *Miklagardr* ('great city'), which was later anglicised to 'Micklegard'. This metropolis on the Golden Horn peninsula in the Bosphorus, with its mighty stone walls and magnificent cathedrals, over which towered the Hagia Sophia, and with its glittering imperial court and exotic bazaars, appeared to the northern visitors like an otherworldly reward for their long and hazardous voyage.

More than anything else, Byzantium was the great port of passage for the trade and wealth of the eastern Mediterranean, from North Africa and from greater Asia. The huge variety of goods ranged from silk fabrics, through exotic fruit, select wines and spices to elegant items of jewellery. Many of the Scandinavians stayed here, enlisted as mercenaries and fought in the imperial army. In the late tenth century the emperor himself was protected

Byzantium, modern Istanbul, built on a peninsula in the Bosphorus, was one of the greatest cities in the medieval world. It was the capital of the eastern Roman empire, and the meeting point of trade routes from the eastern Mediterranean, North Africa and the great expanses of Asia.

by a bodyguard of Vikings, or *Varangoi* as he called them. One of these mercenaries, paid in silver coin, may have been the same Halfdan who scratched his name in Runic characters on the walls of the Hagia Sophia. One of the most famous Norsemen in the imperial bodyguard later ruled Norway as king Harald Hardrada (1015–66). He invaded Northumberland in 1066 and was defeated and slain at the Battle of Stamford Bridge by the Anglo-Saxon king, Harold Godwinson, who was to lose his own life a few weeks later at the Battle of Hastings. Earlier, Harald Hardrada had conducted campaigns as far afield as Italy and Burgundy, in his capacity as a Byzantine general, and is even said to have had an affair with the emperor's wife.

AS FAR AS THE CASPIAN SEA

Whereas most of the Swedish Vikings took the river route through Russia to the Black Sea, several groups of merchants (and probably their families too) ventured further east. After crossing Lake Ladoga, these travellers went overland to the Upper Volga, and finally reached the Caspian Sea.

It was at a market town named Bolgar that the Scandinavians first encountered the large shipments of silver from the Arab world. From AD 750, when the Abbasid caliphs came to power in Baghdad, they had large silver-mines at their disposal. The silver trade with the caliphs gradually died out during the ninth century, when the mines became uneconomic and the caliphate was exhausted by civil war, foreign campaigns and costly building projects. The demand for silver was immeasurable, as evidenced by the more than 60,000 coins found in over a thousand hoards in Scandinavia. We can be sure that the Vikings melted down a proportion of these coins and cast them into ingots or ornamentation. The Vikings received silver in Byzantium in payment for, among other things, furs, slaves, falcons, honey and wax.

From the market at Bolgar the Volga route entered the land of the nomadic Khazars and reached their capital, Itil, on the Caspian Sea. Itil was the terminus of the Silk Road from China. Here Scandinavian merchants met the silk caravans and brought fabrics back to Sweden, where fragments of silk have been found in graves at Birka.

Like Staraya Ladoga, Novgorod and Kiev, many other settlements in the early realm of Rus attest to the presence of Scandinavians and thus underline the importance of rivers as a means of long-distance transport. Thus, from the shores of the North Sea a far-flung transport and trading network extended across the Baltic and up the Russian rivers.

In his chronicle, Olaus Magnus describes the life of the Vikings: hunting, fishing, dragging boats overland and trading.

Evidence of these journeys by the Vikings is also found in the Runic inscriptions they left behind. Some of these are found on a group of thirty stones in central Sweden. These Ingvar Stones mention the helmsmen, ships' captains and navigators who took part in an expedition under the command of Ingvar. The inscriptions also recall Ingvar's brother Harald, in whose memory a stone was erected by his grieving mother. Ingvar is said to have been only 25 years old when he crossed the expanses of Russia with his little fleet in 1036 and may even have pushed on as far as Asia. The sources shed no light on the exact route he took. All we can be sure of is that it ended in disaster, from which only a few survivors returned home. On the Ingvar stone found in the Swedish castle of Gripsholm, we read:

Tola had this stone erected [in memory of]
her son Harald, Ingvar's brother.
They manfully voyaged afar in search of gold.
In the east they gave [food] to the eagle.
They died in the south, in Serkland [land of silk, land of the Saracens].

7 EARLY EXPLORERS:
THE VIKINGS IN THE NORTH ATLANTIC

THE NORWEGIAN SEA AND THE NORTH ATLANTIC

The scarcity of land in Norway suitable for habitation and cultivation was probably what gave the impetus for the many Viking voyages to Scotland and across the Norwegian Sea and the North Atlantic to Iceland and Greenland. In these large and stormy expanses of sea, such voyages were very risky undertakings, and the Nordic sagas expressly emphasise the daring of these first crossing, though later passages across the North Atlantic scarcely seem to merit a mention.

In order to reach places like the Orkneys, Iceland and Greenland, it was necessary to leave the coast of Norway far behind and cross a large expanse of open sea. The seafarers claimed for themselves the territories they had discovered and settled them. From western Norway to the Faroes is a distance of some 675 km (about 365 nautical miles) and to Iceland a further 450 km (240 n.m.). From western Iceland to the nearest point on the east coast of Greenland is 700 km (378 n.m.), and onwards to the south-western corner of Greenland, a further 800 km (432 n.m.). To make a landfall on the far side of the ocean, it was essential to have experienced seaman on highly seaworthy ships capable of carrying an increasing quantity of men, livestock and supplies. A cargo ship of this kind from the period around AD 1000 has been recovered from the Skuldelev ship-barrage north of Roskilde, on the

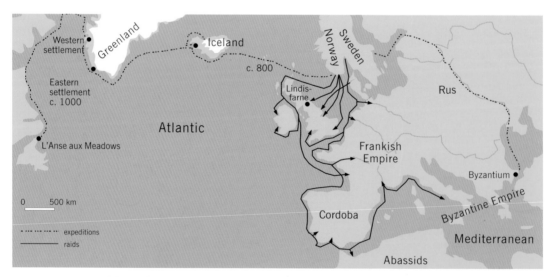

Whether on voyages of trade and exploration, or campaigns of plunder, the Vikings reached almost every corner of the known world and discovered new lands.

Danish island of Sjaeland. The so-called 'Wreck 1' is 16.3 m long, 4.5 m wide and 2 m high amidships; it has a cargo capacity of 40 tons and was probably built in western Norway. When ships of this type reached their destination after a North Atlantic crossing lasting many weeks, they were in a poor state of repair and the crews were exhausted. Indeed, many vessels never reached their objective at all.

However, the first people to explore the islands of the North Atlantic were not Vikings at all but Irish monks. One of these was Dicuil, who was writing in France in AD 825. In his book on the measurement of the circumference of the earth, *Liber de mensura orbis terrae*, Dicuil tells us that from 700 onwards fearless monks were in the habit of crossing the waters in their fragile vessels. We may assume that they crossed the sea in leather boats and settled on the islands as hermits. The Norsemen, who encountered these monks in the Faroes and Iceland, called them *papar* – 'fathers'. The Vikings' fearsome appearance boded ill for the monks who fled as soon as they arrived, leaving behind them their books, bells and crooks – as the Icelandic historian Ari Thorgilsson wrote in about 1120.

THE ORKNEYS AND SHETLANDS

Among the first groups of islands reached by the Norwegian Vikings in their oceangoing voyages were the Orkneys and Shetlands, lying north of Scotland's north-eastern tip. At the time of the Vikings' arrival, the islands were already settled by Picts, a race that had inhabited Scotland even before the Celts. There are indications of peaceful coexistence, but also signs of violent disputes. Before the Vikings had established permanent settlements in the Orkneys, they had launched seaborne raids on the islands, as can be gathered from a passage from the Saga of King Olaf the Holy (*Olafs saga helga*, of about 1230): 'It is told that in the days of Harald the Fair-haired, King of Norway [c. 870–940], the Orkney islands were settled, which previously had mainly been a gathering-place for the Vikings.'

However, the exact date of the settlement is in dispute. The era of actual Viking presence in the Orkneys – commonly placed between the first raids in the eighth century and the tenth century – is only a relatively short period in the long age of Scandinavian influence. According to the *Orkneyinga Saga*, a county was founded there in 874, thus apparently bringing the pillaging to an end. We read:

In one summer Harald the Fair-haired sailed to the west, in order to punish the Vikings, because he had become weary of their pillaging, since they plundered Norway during the summer, but spent their winters in the Orkneys and Shetlands... he fought many battles there and annexed land further to the west than any king has done since then. In one battle Ivar, the son of Jarl [earl] Rognvald, fell. But when King Harald sailed home from the west, he handed over the Shetlands and Orkneys to Jarl Rognvald as compensation for his son. However, Jarl Rognvald gave both lands to his brother Sigurd.

Admittedly, the saga was written at a later date (c. 1200), yet the appointment of *jarls*, who were usually connected to the Norwegian royal house, as governors, marks the beginning of direct political control from Norway. However, the power of the *jarls* was limited, since individual warlords certainly continued their pillaging raids for some time to come.

During the period of colonisation, the Norwegian settlers found in the Orkneys a landscape which, though not dissimilar to that of northern Scandinavia, enjoyed a milder climate. That is why the islands, like the Shetlands lying to the north-east of them, were very attractive to Norse settlers.

Little is known about the early settlement of the Shetland islands. Traces of the first phase of Viking settlement have been found in Jarlshof on the main island, today an important archaeological site. The complex of buildings is part of a group of structures from different periods, going back as far as the Bronze Age. From Norse times there are dwelling houses, barns and stables. Like their counterparts in Norway, these were built with thick walls of turfs.

ICELAND

From the Faroe islands the Norsemen sailed on to Iceland, in the middle of the North Atlantic. Depending on the winds, it could have taken anything from a week to a month to reach Iceland from Norway, probably calling at the Shetlands and Faroes on the way. Nearly three-quarters of this barren and inhospitable island was, and is, made up of volcanic mountains, lava-fields and glaciers. The only arable land was to be found on the coastal rim and in the valleys of the south and south-west. Once again it is the Irish monk, Dicuil, who has left behind a detailed description:

It is now thirty years since men of the church [clerici], who had lived on the island from first day of February to the first day of August, told me that, not only on the day of the summer solstice but also on the days before and after it, the setting sun appeared only to dip behind a low hill, so that during this period it never became dark. Rather could a man do anything he wished, even to search for lice in his shirt, just as well as in broad daylight. Those who describe the sea all around the island as frozen, are in error… yet if they set out from the island and sail northwards for one day they do find the sea frozen.

This and other accounts of northern voyages by Celtic saints such as St Brendan, lead us to the conclusion that some sixty to seventy years before the arrival of the Vikings a settlement already existed on Thule, the Roman name for Iceland. So far, there have been no archaeological finds pointing to a settlement earlier than the ninth century, that is to say before the arrival of the Norsemen. The official record of Norse colonisation (the *Landnamabok*, dating from later than 1200) tells us that Iceland was definitely claimed by one Ingolf in AD 874. However, we should assume today that this book was not really a record of actual events but was rather intended to secure and legitimise the occupations of land in the twelfth and thirteenth centuries. When Ingolf sighted land after a long voyage – so the *Landnamabok* tells us – he apparently threw the decorative wooden supports of his throne-like chair into the sea. At the point where they were washed up on the shore he established his settlement. This gives us a description – albeit legendary – of the founding of the town we know today as Reykjavik.

In contrast to the Shetlands or Faroes, Iceland was colonised, in the view of the medieval chroniclers, because independent farmers were driven out by the policy of subjugation imposed by the Norwegian king, Harald the Fair-haired. However, not all the early settlers came from Norway, but also from Britain and Ireland. As well as repression in their home countries, it was probably the shortage of land that was decisive in compelling these people to embark on the dangerous voyage across the North Atlantic. Settlement was concentrated in the coastal areas and the broad valleys.

The book of colonisation mentions, for example, some 430 'land-takers' or colonists (*landsnamsmenn*), male and female, who were the first to settle and cultivate the land, mainly in the southern plain and in fjord valleys in other parts of the island. Some sixty years after the colonisation, in other words around AD 930, Iceland was completely settled if we are to believe the historical record. It is difficult to determine the number and proportion of the settlers from different countries of origin, but it is estimated that 20,000 people crossed the sea to Iceland, and that this population grew to around 60,000. Every inch of fertile soil had soon been occupied by the original Nordic farmers; later arrivals were only left with poorer land. One of those was the outlawed killer, Erik the Red.

GREENLAND

Erik the Red is described in a few sentences by Ari Thorgilsson in 'The Book of the Icelanders', in around 1125. They come at the beginning of his account of one of the most astonishing sea voyages of medieval times, on which Erik set out in 985 or 986, shortly before Iceland was converted to Christianity in 1000:

> *The land which is called Greenland was discovered and settled from Iceland. Erik the Red was the name of the man... he gave the land the name of Greenland; he thought that it would make men desirous to go there, if the land had such a beautiful name.*

In 970 Erik had quit a region of south-western Norway that had been densely populated for a thousand years, had then established a farm in Iceland and there, on account of a number of murders, so the sources tell us, had been declared an outlaw. That is why he left Iceland in 982 in search of the fabled islands of Gunnbjørn, lying across the Atlantic to the west. After three years of voyages that took him in the wrong direction, he finally came upon a land whose east coast, with its sheer cliffs and ice-cap, appeared uninhabitable, but which in the south-west offered something he had found in Iceland: large expanses of grassland dotted with dwarf birches and willows, on plains and gentle slopes leading to the sheltered upper reaches of fjords – it was indeed a green land. The name has been called the greatest confidence-trick of all time, yet visitors to Greenland in summer are astonished at how much green is to be seen around the fjords and in the plains of the southern interior. Between the sea, the inhospitable west coast and the glaciers in the east, the grasslands along the fjords offered subsistence for the communities of settlers. In the *Kongespejlet* ('The Mirror of Kings'), a Norwegian document from the first half of the thirteenth century, there is an account of the Greenland farmsteads:

> *... that in Greenland there are good pastures, and large, fine farmsteads, for there they have livestock and many sheep and they make much butter and cheese; from this they chiefly live, and likewise from meat, fish and game of all kinds, as well as reindeer meat and the meat of whale, seal and bear.*

When his term of outlawry had expired, Erik returned to Iceland in 985, and took his family and quite a number of settlers to Greenland on 25 ships. Sadly, after a voyage of many weeks and a distance of 1,300 km (over 700 n.m.) only

14 of the ships reached the new colony, as we learn from the *Landnamabok* and the Saga of Erik the Red (*Eiriks Saga Rauda)* from the second half of the thirteenth century.

VINLAND-AMERICA

The sagas give accounts of another adventure at sea. They tell us that Bjarne Herjulfsson was a young lad of 20. After a summer stay in Norway, he spent the autumn in Iceland, where he learned that his father had gone away to Greenland. Bjarne set off immediately in pursuit of him. After three days of good sailing weather a storm arose and his ship was blown off course. After another four days the sun came out again. Bjarne and his crew sailed further westward. When they finally sighted land, they realised that it was not Greenland since there were no high cliffs or glaciers. Instead the coast, with its low hills, looked hospitable. Bjarne sailed further along the coast and later sighted a forested region; then after two more days he turned round and set a course for Greenland.

The son of Erik the Red, Leif Erikson, heard about what Bjarne had seen and in 992 fitted out a ship, with a crew of 35 men, for a voyage westwards from Greenland. Eventually Leif reached an island with glaciers and a barren coast, which he called *Helluland.* Much later it was renamed Baffin Island. He sailed on and came to low-lying, forested land with white beaches, which he named *Markland* (now Labrador). Finally he came to a land that he named *Vinland* (now Newfoundland). Here he proposed to spend the winter, since there was enough grass to feed the livestock brought on board, and timber to build houses. In the rivers and the sea swam salmon that were larger than those in Norway. The winter climate was mild and the grass scarcely wilted. Even the lengths of day and night were more equally balanced than in Greenland. After wintering there, with the arrival of spring Leif sailed back to Greenland.

Back in Iceland and Norway the account of this voyage aroused lively interest. Thorvald Erikson, Leif's brother, advocated the exploration of a larger area. Leif proposed that his brother should sail west again in the same ships. Thorvald took 30 men on the trip and wintered in Vinland. The following summer was spent in exploring more of the coastline, and the ship returned to Vinland for a second winter. Setting off on a new voyage in the spring, Thorvald reached a wooded promontory, which he thought would be very suitable for building a homestead. However, dangers lurked in this attractive country. Fighting broke out with the warlike indigenous people, whom the Norsemen called *Skraelinger*, in the course of which Thorvald was fatally wounded.

The sad news reached Greenland, but the undertaking was not abandoned, and the Norsemen decided to settle the new land. The third expedition to Vinland, led by Thorfinn Karlsefni, was fitted out. Thorfinn was a man of great wealth, who had spent the winter with Leif Erikson at his farm called Brattahlid. The Greenland Saga goes on to tell of a group of some 160 new settlers, including women, who set out for Vinland. They also took livestock with them, a further indication that they intended to found a colony. After an uneventful voyage they spent the winter in Vinland. Even the native inhabitants appeared friendly. Their main interest was in trading furs for the weapons of the Vikings. but they were satisfied enough with milk from cows – a phenomenon unknown to them. However, after another winter, hostilities broke out again with the natives, several of whom were killed. The Norsemen spent a final winter there and then – no doubt fearing further battles with the more numerous natives – set off on the return voyage to Greenland. The last expedition mentioned in the saga led to an equally brief sojourn in North America owing to quarrelling among the settlers.

Archaeological research on the northern tip of Newfoundland has discovered relics of the Norse settlement. On the southern shore of a bay is a place called l'Anse aux Meadows, where traces of the short-lived Scandinavian settlement have been found. Sharpened stakes lodged in skeletons bear witness to battles with the indigenous people. Vinland was the furthest point reached by the Norsemen on their voyages. Without knowing it, they had discovered a new continent.

THE END OF THE VIKING SETTLEMENTS IN GREENLAND

While the Icelandic colony prospered and the country has since become a successful independent republic populated by the descendants of those Scandinavian pioneers, the settlement of Greenland was not successful in the long term. There are written historical records of the colony up to 1408, after which settlements seem to have died out there. Increasing cold, disease and perhaps also hostilities with the indigenous Inuit, destroyed the meagre basis of subsistence for the Norsemen, who remained dependent on links with the Iceland and Europe. When a Norwegian ship, commanded by Hans Egede, reached Greenland again in 1721, he found the settlement abandoned. Nonetheless, the Viking voyagers, setting out from Norway, had opened up the entire North Atlantic. While the Norsemen were peaceful colonisers of Iceland and Greenland, on other populated coasts they became the terror from the sea, whenever their square sails appeared unexpectedly on the horizon.

8 'TERRIBLE PORTENTS': VIKING EXPEDITIONS OF PILLAGE AND CONQUEST

ENGLAND

In this year [AD 793] terrible portents appeared over Northumbria and miserably frightened the inhabitants: these were exceptional flashes of lightning, and fiery dragons were seen flying in the air. A great famine followed these signs; and a little after that, in the same year on 8 June, the harrying of the heathen miserably destroyed God's church in Lindisfarne by rapine and slaughter.[1]

105

VIKING
EXPEDITIONS
OF PILLAGE
AND
CONQUEST

What this fearful account from the Anglo-Saxon Chronicle describes is the first historically documented assault on the English coast by men who were presumably Norwegian Vikings. We can imagine the terror felt by the monks of Lindisfarne Abbey, off the coast of Northumberland, when they saw a number of square-sailed ships on the horizon, approaching rapidly. As they watched, men who seemed like fierce barbarians, leapt ashore, plundered and pillaged everything they could find and set fire to the monastery.

There had been earlier contacts between Scandinavia and Britain, but now began an endless series of sudden assaults, followed by larger-scale invasions. As early as 792, King Offa of Mercia, a realm embracing much of central and southern England, had ordered defences to be built on the south coast against heathen warriors whom he did not identify more closely. As news of these lightning attacks spread through England, the reaction was doubtless one of horror and panic. Shortly after the destruction of Lindisfarne Abbey, together with the church dedicated to St Cuthbert, the monk and adviser to Charlemagne, Alcuin, wrote in a letter full of reproach:

Never before has there been such terror in Britain, as we have now suffered at the hands of a heathen people, and never has it been thought possible that such a hostile assault could be mounted from the sea. Lo, the church of St Cuthbert is besmirched with the blood of God's priests and robbed of all its ornaments; a place that is more venerable than any other in Britain has become prey to heathens.

---

1 Translated by Elaine Traherne in *Legacy of the Vikings*, 2001.

The pillaging of the monastery of Lindisfarne, off the north-east coast of England, ushered in the period of Viking raids. Today only ruins of the monastery remain.

A year after the destruction of Lindisfarne, a second monastery in Northumbria, either Monkwearmouth or Jarrow, was burnt down in a Viking attack. After that, the attacks were concentrated on Ireland. For the next thirty years England could sleep more easily. But then even worse befell the island. After successful landings on the Friesian coast of what are now the Netherlands, a large Danish force landed on the island of Sheppey on the south shore of the Thames estuary. In the years that followed, the south coast of England was subject to repeated attacks.

Behind the plunderers and invaders mentioned in the English sources may be concealed men of varied origin, organisation and leadership. The ships involved in the first attacks may have carried high-ranking leaders and their retinues, but it is also possible that groups of well-armed landowners could have banded together in order to augment their income. Runic stones tell of such aggression even in Scandinavia.

In the year 850 the Norsemen changed their strategy. Hitherto, the campaigns had been seasonal; they plundered in summer and returned in their ships to Scandinavia for the winter. Their success depended on the manoeuvrability of their shallow-draught vessels. This enabled them to go up rivers deep into the interior, carry out lightning attacks and, before a superior force could be mustered to retaliate, to retreat with their booty. However, in 850, for the first time, a Viking force spent the winter in Thanet. In the next few years onslaught followed onslaught, and the Anglo-Saxon kingdom sought to buy off the enemy by payment of the 'Danegeld'. Even this did not always prove successful, as we read in the Anglo-Saxon Chronicle for the year 865:

> *Under the cover of this peace-treaty and the promise of money, the army stole secretly inland by night and laid waste to the whole of eastern Kent.*

At first there was no organised structure to the attacks, but this changed after 865. Where previously the Chronicles spoke of no more than 23 ships, now numbers ranging from 80 to 350 are quoted, with likely fighting crews of between 30 and 60 warriors. Confronting these armoured Scandinavian troops and their auxiliaries, there were usually no more than some hastily mustered Anglo-Saxon peasants. The outcome was obvious. The first region to fall into Viking hands was Northumbria, in 866. Here the principal gateway for shipping was the Humber. The ancient Roman city of York, which of course stood on the Ouse, a tributary of the Humber, now became a Danish stronghold. Excavations in York's Coppergate reveal three phases of Scandinavian settlement, dating from the ninth to the eleventh centuries. However, the finds are evidence not just of plunder but of extensive trading links. From York, the Anglo-Saxon kingdoms of East Anglia and Mercia were overrun in subsequent campaigns, and finally Wessex as well. But in 878, King Alfred the Great, who had fled further west, succeeded in reconquering Wessex and Mercia. Nevertheless, for some time to come, the north and east of England remained under Danish rule, and was named the Danelaw.

107

VIKING
EXPEDITIONS
OF PILLAGE
AND
CONQUEST

Along the Thames and other rivers numerous fortified towns or *burhs* were built as an effective defence against the Danes. Sometimes use was made of Iron Age or Roman forts, while elsewhere they were newly built. In many cases the defences protected river fords (e.g. Chelmsford, Guildford, Oxford). At the same time they served as centres of trade and administration.

Finally, in 954 the kingdom of Mercia succeeded in reconquering the Danelaw. We will not examine these campaigns in more detail, since they were for the most part fought on land and belong to a period when surprise raids by the Vikings were already a thing of the past.

IRELAND AND THE IRISH SEA

Like the coasts of England, the neighbouring island of Ireland was the target of numerous raids and of planned colonisation. At the northern entrance to the Irish Sea lay the Isle of Man. The 655 m (2,000 ft) mountain in the north of the island could be seen from a long way off, and since it was snow-covered in winter, the Norsemen called it Snaefell, the name it still bears today. To judge from archaeological evidence, it seems that Vikings occupied the island and subjugated the indigenous Christian population. However, written sources tell us nothing of this. Of the Viking ships active in the Irish sea from AD 790 onwards, some struck at the coast of Wales, while others sailed to Ireland. Wales became a permanent element in the western sea route and a port of call for trading vessels. This is confirmed by buried hordes of silver and coins found near the coast. Furthermore, the *Annals of Ulster*, written in the fifteenth century, tell us that in Dublin in the tenth and eleventh centuries merchants were trading in Welsh slaves, horses, honey and corn.

These annals also give an account of the first Viking raid on Irish soil in the year 795, at a place called Rechru, which is probably the island of Rathlin, off the northern Irish coast. The raids followed a familiar pattern. In the second decade of the ninth century there were isolated attacks, then in 830 the invaders pushed inland and in 839 an army wintered there for the first time. Soon after that, in 841 the Vikings founded Dublin.

THE EMPIRE OF THE FRANKS

In this period, other Norse fleets sailed along what is now the northern coast of France, then part of the Frankish empire, where they terrorised the population. The following account was left by the Frankish monk, Ermentarius of Noirmoutier:

The number of ships is growing: the endless stream of Vikings swells without cease. Everywhere the Christians are the victims of massacres, burnings and pillage. The Vikings seize everything that lies in their path, and no-one offers any resistance. They capture Bordeaux, Périgueux, Limoges, Angoulême and Toulouse. The towns of Anger, Tours and Orléans are obliterated. A fleet of innumerable ships sails up the Seine, and the evil spreads throughout the region. Rouen is laid waste, plundered and burned. Paris, Beauvais and Meaux are taken. The mighty fortress of Melun is razed to the ground, Chartres occupied, Evreux and Bayeux plundered and every town besieged.

109

VIKING

EXPEDITIONS

OF PILLAGE

AND

CONQUEST

Though at first the Vikings only carried out sporadic raids, in the second half of the ninth century they attacked Britain with large, well-organised armies.

The *Historia Anglorum* of Matthew Paris tells of King Alfred's struggle against the Vikings.

These marauding campaigns followed a pattern similar to that in Britain. The Viking ships used rivers as gateways to the interior. Often the raids took place alternately on either side of the English Channel. In order to stop the Vikings, Charlemagne issued decrees that river bridges should be fortified against the fleets. This was the only way open for a land-based power, which had no ships to deploy against the Norse fleets. In the unsettled times following the death of Charlemagne's son Ludwig the Pious in 841, two large Viking fleets were operating in France, one on the Seine, the other on the Loire. The Vikings also attacked the Friesian lands and, as we have seen, destroyed the port of Dorestad on more than one occasion. They had a fortified base for their fleet on the island of Walcheren, strategically situated at the mouth of the Scheldt. From 838 onwards, the raids shifted further west and south, along the Channel and Atlantic coasts of France. After the mid-ninth century the highly manoeuvrable Viking fleets no longer just sailed up the French rivers every summer, but two sizeable armies spent the winter there, as they did in England.

Through a combination of quick raids on wealthy monasteries, establishing trading posts and settlements, and extorting protection money in the manner of the Danegeld, the Viking armies could roam the country freely, feeding and supplying themselves. The powerlessness of the Frankish rulers against these attacks is underlined by legal documents and property-deeds from the tenth century. The only means of defence was to set Vikings against Vikings. For example, a Norseman named Harald settled in Friesland where he received a land-grant from Ludwig the Pious in 826. His brother was the same Rorik who had been placed in charge of Dorestad, with the task of protecting the coast of Friesland.

111

VIKING
EXPEDITIONS
OF PILLAGE
AND
CONQUEST

Normandy

The Frankish king Karl (Charles) III (879–929), nicknamed 'The Simple', made an offer to the Vikings operating on the Seine, that he would grant them land if they would defend it against other attacks. Their Norwegian commander, named in the Frankish sources as Rollo, and in the later Nordic sagas as *Gøngu-Hrólfr*, 'Rolf the Swift', was accordingly granted territory in what is now eastern Normandy. Although Rollo initially maintained order, his followers were soon forcing their way up the rivers on plundering forays deep into France. When, in 924, Rollo handed power over to his son, William Longsword, he had subjugated a large part of Normandy. In 933 William completed his conquest by seizing the Cotentin peninsula.

The settling of Normandy by the Vikings has left scarcely any recognisable archaeological traces. One exception is the fortified complex with earth ramparts near La Hague at the tip of the Cotentin peninsula, probably the site of a Viking stronghold in the tenth century. Scandinavian swords, axes and spearheads have been found in the rivers, confirming the violent character of that age. However, we should not overlook the fact that the Norsemen very soon intermarried and merged with the indigenous population.

Brittany

In Brittany, too, the coast was prey to Viking attacks, while from the landward side the hitherto independent country occupied by Celtic Bretons was conquered by one of Charlemagne's armies. The Viking ships followed the much-travelled route west around Brittany's hazardous extremities, Ushant and Finisterre, and then south-east to the mouth of the Loire. There, from 836 onward, the island monastery of Noirmoutier provided a base for the invaders – this was the home of the monk Ermentarius, whose invective against the Vikings was quoted earlier.

In the early tenth century these attacks intensified, until by 914 the entire region was occupied by Norwegian Vikings. However, this occupation differed from the others, in that it was purely dedicated to pillage and plunder; there is no evidence of trade or agriculture. The Breton nobility and the clergy fled to England, to the court of King Athelstan. However, in the long run Brittany could not be held down by force. With English support an exiled Breton leader organised a seaborne invasion. A circular fort was recently discovered at Péran near St Brieuc on the north coast of Brittany, but it is not clear whether this was attacked or defended by a Scandinavian force. However, another three years would pass before the last Vikings were driven out of Brittany.

The brief occupation of Brittany has nonetheless left behind one extraordinary archaeological find. On the small island of Groix, off the south coast of Brittany, a magnificent boat-grave was erected in the first half of the tenth century. It appears that a long-ship, accompanied by a tender, was dragged along a processional way lined with standing stones, to the place where it was to be buried. Numerous grave-gifts such as weapons, harness, gold and silver ornaments, dice made from walrus-teeth, blacksmith's tools and agricultural implements, were laid out with the bodies of an adult and an adolescent male in a ship surrounded by 24 shields. Then the ship was burned and the ashes covered over by a mound of earth – bearing impressive witness to a Viking culture that was wedded to the sea.

Despite a few sporadic raids lasting into the eleventh century, this was the end of the age of the great Scandinavian fleets. However, with the establishment of the Duchy of Normandy a Scandinavian presence was retained on the European mainland.

The great distance these daring Norsemen sailed on the marauding forays is shown by their voyages southward along the Atlantic coast. Some even took their ships as far as Spain. Thus in 859 Bjørn Ironside and Hastein led a fleet through the Straits of Gibraltar into the Mediterranean, where they spent two years plundering the coasts of North Africa, southern France and Italy, before returning in 862 to their base on the Loire. However, the resistance put up by the Arabs in North Africa deterred other Norsemen from imitating Ironside and Hastein. Yet it was not only the coasts of the western Mediterranean that were threatened by the men who now called themselves Normans. On at least two occasions war-fleets manned by Scandinavians from Kiev reached the walls of Constantinople. Once a prince of Rus nailed a shield on the gates of the city to demonstrate his contempt for the might of the emperor. However, capturing the great city would have been unthinkable.

113

VIKING

EXPEDITIONS

OF PILLAGE

AND

CONQUEST

The last phase of Viking expansion coincides with the creation of organised forms of state in Denmark and Norway in the tenth to eleventh centuries. After the last Viking ruler had been driven out of York in 954, raiding began anew in 980. At the same time sporadic attacks were carried out on the Welsh coast from Viking centres in Ireland. The great fleets which, under royal commanders, set out from Norway against England, were well-organised fighting forces. In 991, Olaf Tryggvason, who was crowned king of Norway in 995, led a fleet of 93 ships to the south-east coast of England. However, these Vikings, some of whom were from Sweden, soon met with resistance and so accepted payment of Danegeld as a compromise. In the years that followed, the sums the victims had to pay for their liberty grew ever greater: in 1002 the total was 11,800 kg (some 12 *tons*) of silver, and in 1012 no less than 22 tons. This wealth in turn served to increase the power of the Scandinavian monarchies. So it is no surprise that the Danish king Sven (or Sweyn) Forkbeard gave serious thought to an invasion of England.

Soon after the death of the king, his successor Knut (or Canute) succeeded in incorporating northern and central England into his realm, which also encompassed the whole of Denmark, Norway and Sweden. However, after his death this empire of the north fell apart.

The Norwegian Harald Hardrada, who saw himself as Knut's successor,

Through pillage and tributes like the Danegeld, vast quantities of silver and jewellery came into the hands of the Vikings, as can be seen today in burials and unearthed hoards of treasure.

attempted once again to establish his supremacy around the North Sea. Having gained experience in endless campaigns against Denmark, he kept his plans secret. The English king, Harold Godwinson – himself of Viking descent – was taken completely by surprise when, in 1066, a Norwegian fleet of 200 ships sailed up the Humber estuary and landed at Ricall on the river Ouse. The Norwegian king had been encouraged to launch this campaign by Harold's brother, Tostig, who had been banished from England a year before. The fleets of Tostig and the Jarl of the Orkneys now joined the invasion force, which may have totalled 300 ships and 9,000 warriors. York and the coastal area quickly fell under Hardrada's control. With his army he pressed southward some 22 km (13 miles). When the Norwegian king set up camp at Stamford Bridge, something unexpected happened. In great haste Harold Godwinson had assembled an army and made a forced march northwards to meet the surprised invaders. After a day of brutal combat Godwinson was victorious, and the Norwegian king was killed by an arrow in the throat, while leading an attack. All night the English pursued the invaders back to their ships. Only 24 vessels returned carrying the wounded to Norway. The last attempt at conquest by the Scandinavian Vikings had failed.

115

VIKING

EXPEDITIONS

OF PILLAGE

AND

CONQUEST

Yet Harold Godwinson was not to enjoy the fruits of victory for long. For Duke William of Normandy, also descended from the Norsemen who had settled there, had been forging similar plans for conquest. The same wind that had carried the Norwegian fleet to the coast of Yorkshire at first kept the Norman ships storm-bound in Dieppe on the Channel coast. When the fleet finally set sail on 27 September, Harald Hardrada had already fallen at Stamford Bridge. Once over the Channel, the Norman army was able to land unopposed on the Sussex coast and began to establish a fortified position.

After the Battle of Stamford Bridge, the English army marched the 400 km (240 miles) south in just four days. With no time to recover their strength, the force of some 7,000 peasant soldiers reached an area near Hastings. William's forces were numerically no larger, but they included several hundred bowmen and troops of armoured horsemen. The two armies clashed on 14 October 1066 near Hastings, at a place where the village was later named Battle. The Battle of Hastings has been famously and impressively captured in one of the best-known pictorial sources – the Bayeux Tapestry. The English army was arrayed along the crest of a hill, from where a good view could be obtained of the marshy valley where the Normans were positioned. At the centre of Harold's army was his bodyguard with the dragon banner of Wessex. In the misty light of dawn the Norman forces began to advance. But their horses slithered in the morass, and from the high ground a hail of spears, branches and stones drummed down on

The Bayeux Tapestry depicts the landing in England by William the Conqueror in 1066, and the Battle of Hastings.

the foot-soldiers. When they retreated, panic broke out. The Breton contingent fled and dragged some of the Norman troops with them. Anticipating victory, the English army pursued the fleeing enemy and left the safety of their ridge. However, William succeeded in rallying his troops and now deployed his superior armoured cavalry, who cut down half of Harold's foot-soldiers in the valley. The English were forced to retreat to their ridge. For the final battle the bodyguard close ranks around their king, Harold. First his brothers were killed, then the king himself was struck down by an arrow in his eye (according to the Tapestry). In the same year William of Normandy, soon to be known as William the Conqueror, was crowned king of England in Westminster Abbey.

William's invasion was the last time a seaborne landing on English soil succeeded against opposition.[2] After decades of warfare, the Norwegians, Swedes and Danes were so exhausted that there were no further fleet operations on a grand scale. In 1069 a Danish fleet came to support an Anglo-Saxon uprising in the north, but William defeated the rebels and bought off the Danish interlopers. As late as the thirteenth century there was a last isolated episode when Norwegian ships raided the coast of Ireland.

---

[2] The landing in 1688 by William of Orange with an army at Torbay was unopposed; King James II fled the country almost immediately, and William, whose claim to the throne was legitimate, succeeded him in a peaceful transition.

9 A MEDIEVAL SEA POWER?
THE HANSEATIC LEAGUE

THE ORIGINS OF THE HANSEATIC LEAGUE

Even today the number-plates of German cars from Hamburg, Bremen and Lübeck display an 'H' for *Hansestadt* before the initial letter of the city – HH for Hamburg, HB for Bremen and HL for Lübeck. *Hansa* is the German term for what the English-speaking world calls the Hanseatic League. But what exactly is or was the 'Hansa'? It is remembered as an alliance of medieval cities and a maritime power, but the reality was rather different. The word *Hansa* originally meant a community or fellowship, but in the High Middle Ages it came to refer to a large association of itinerant merchants. The first known documentary reference to *Hansa Alman(ie)* (German Hansa) dates from 1282. Around the middle of the fourteenth century we can increasingly recognise a sense of fellowship and common interest among Low German merchants. Until then, trade was largely governed by merchants from Gotland, who were organised into formal associations.

Trade and mercantile guilds in pre-Hanseatic times

Until the mid-twelfth century German merchants from the cities of the Lower Rhine, Westphalia and Lower Saxony, who wished to trade internationally in the Baltic, had no choice but to do so on ships whose home ports lay outside the German (Holy Roman) Empire. For the whole of the south coast of the Baltic was settled by Slavs. In the north, German merchants had access to Schleswig, which since the mid-eleventh century had supplanted Hedeby as the regional entrepôt. Here the ships moored at wharves. As well as in Schleswig, Low German merchants also settled in Old Lübeck. At these ports they could trade their goods – products from central Europe such as cloth, utensils, jewellery and wine – in return for natural commodities from the north such as furs, honey, wax and amber. It is possible that some merchants ventured into the Baltic region on board ships.

The major part of the trade between Schleswig and the chief suppliers of products from Russia and Scandinavia was brokered by the landowning entrepreneurs of Gotland. Most of the goods changed hands several times before reaching the final customer. This was to the advantage of the ports through which the commerce passed: they compelled the visiting merchants to transfer their wares to local ships or wagons and even to offer them for sale at the market, in order to extract some revenue from them.

The trade was in the hands of merchants who formed themselves into associations and thus increased their influence. These companies of merchants with common interests offered more protection when they travelled, especially abroad. In an age when there were no passports, their members possessed a form of common identity, and their shared origins and legal customs created a basis for joint action. By combining forces when in a foreign town, they were better placed to complain if cheated in money-changing, or with false weights and measures, and with similar problems. In this way the Danish overseas traders in certain cities joined together to form *Knudsgilden* (Canute Guilds) modelled on that of Schleswig. We know that in the 1270s there was also a guild of 'Canute Brethren' in Gotland, running the island's commerce. Since they enjoyed the protection of the Danish king, they came into direct competition with the 'Gotland-farers' from Lübeck. Early in their existence, the German association of Gotland-farers possessed their own seal with which to identify their title-deeds and other documents. The Gotland-farers were the first of many other societies or *Hansen* formed by merchants 'of German tongue'.

German strongholds on the south coast of the Baltic

With the increasing German influence on the southern coast of the Baltic, economic and political circumstances changed. The stream of German settlers to this area led to the founding of new towns and cities. In East Prussia and Livonia (roughly modern Latvia) the Teutonic Knights became the ruling power. These formidable crusaders had originally been called in by Duke Konrad of Maszovia (now part of Poland) to assist with the conversion of the still heathen Prussians. This mean that German merchants could now put into new German ports on the Baltic coast and take control of commerce along these routes.

In the thirteenth century German overseas traders, or more precisely their apprentices and factors, made their own way from Lübeck to the Baltic and Russian markets, using Gotland as a port of call. Although Gotland remained the most important entrepôt for trade with Russia and Sweden, the Gotland merchants were, from the early thirteenth century onwards, increasingly forced out of east–west trade by their German competitors. As early as 1184–5 German merchants sailed into the lower reaches of the river Davgava. From Lübeck the sea route ran eastwards via Visby, the main port of Gotland. In the summer months, merchants could sail up the river Narva, which now forms the border between Russia and Estonia, then into the large Lake Peipus, at the southern end of which lay the important trading centre of Pskov. In winter, there is evidence that traders sailed into Riga, at the mouth of the river Daugava, whence they transported their goods on sledges over land to Pskov and probably as far as Novgorod. Overseas traders from Germany also settled in Denmark in the twelfth century. In the thirteenth century ships from Lübeck reached Norway. Here corn from the south was traded for cod and dried fish.

Better harbours and waterways

The harbours of the new towns became the focus of maritime trade. Very often situated on the banks of rivers and some way inland, they offered good protection against storms. Admittedly, the silting up of rivers could cause great problems by making it difficult or impossible for larger ships to enter. Keeping the harbours clear of flotsam and refuse, of wrecks and jettisoned ballast, was essential for the smooth flow of commerce. The first regulations governing this activity date from the Hanseatic period, such as the 1359 *Bursprake* (civic decree) in Hamburg, which forbade the throwing of ballast into the harbour, the drainage creeks and the dammed Alster river.

The network of waterways was improved. For example, in 1398 the Stecknitz Canal was completed linking Lübeck with Lauenberg on the Elbe, providing a direct route between the North Sea and the Baltic. It had locks to ensure sufficient depth of water for shipping throughout its length. Much of the canal was in fact a river that had been narrowed in places to about 5 m, with walls of stone and timber on both sides. Lock gates were held in position by the pressure of water on one side. It generally took about two days for the level of water behind the gates to rise sufficiently to make the stretch navigable. The ships were hauled upstream through the locks by men pulling long ropes. A journey between Lübeck and Hamburg could easily take several weeks.

Expansion of trade

With the improvements in transport and new economic and political circumstances the nature of trade also changed. Not only were goods traded in larger quantities, but their variety was also greater than before. The hitherto customary exchange of luxury goods gave way to import and export in mass volumes. Urban markets and a money economy were the characteristic features of business life in the Hanseatic age. The old trading in goods by merchants who travelled abroad was replaced by a system of permanent commercial premises (*Kontore*).

At fairs in Skåne (Scania), the Danish-occupied south of Sweden, herrings would be bought and sold in huge quantities – at their peak the markets of Skåne turned over 200,000 to 300,000 tons of herring each year. In the rapidly growing towns and cities there was a healthy demand for these fish, and

Technical questions of seaworthiness and safety at sea were taken more seriously in the Hanseatic age. There were now special rules governing port activities. This illuminated manuscript of Hamburg's city laws, dating from 1497, relates to shipping, and shows a dock with a crane loading cargo onto a ship. In the inner harbour boats and small vessels are moored to a quay, and in the background there are seagoing ships, to which freight was carried. This illustrates the arrangements in Hamburg at that time, where there was an inner and an outer harbour, separated by a tree trunk in the water. The loading and unloading of cargoes in the inner harbour was only allowed by permission of the council.

during medieval fasts, salted herring was never off the menu! But large quantities of salt were required for its preservation. Turfs with a high salt content were dug up in sea marshes on the North Sea coasts of England, the Netherlands and North Friesland. However, a better quality of salt was obtained from the salt-pans in places like Lüneburg. From there a salt-road led to Lübeck. From Sweden came timber for building, as well as copper and iron. Another source of timber, as well as grain, were the territories controlled by the Teutonic Knights in East Prussia and Livonia. England supplied wool and Flanders textiles.

In order to transport all these goods by sea, larger ships were needed, as well as good ports and associated infrastructure. The cogs and carracks moored alongside wooden wharves or stone quays, on which cranes were set up to unload the cargoes. Unloading could not start without permission from the council.

The merchants and the cities

In the twelfth and early thirteenth centuries a few individual merchants were still conducting their trade abroad on their own account. This group of merchants was bound by a common origin, legal customs and commercial interests. In the course of the thirteenth century, this changed, with overseas traders staying in their home towns, from where they controlled their foreign negotiations through apprentices and factors. Even barter trade with foreign partners was managed from these city counting-houses. At the same time the

On city councils it was the merchants who set the agenda.

constitution of the cities changed; the council was usually dominated by wealthy merchants, whose money and influenced enabled them to determine policy independently of the princes. Once they had ceased going to sea themselves, they had ample time to take up the office of councillor in their home city. This meant that attending to the common interests of traders in Lower Germany was no longer the task of a brotherhood of merchants operating abroad, but rather of a loose association of cities with trading interests that sometimes coincided. Increasingly the cities reached major decisions within the Hansa itself. Lübeck and Visby, for example, struck up an alliance with Riga in 1280, in which they assumed responsibility for protecting the Germans who travelled regularly to Novgorod – without involving the (Swedish) Gotland Association, which then rapidly lost its importance.

THE LEGAL STATUS OF THE HANSA: MERCHANTS' ASSOCIATION OR LEAGUE OF CITIES?

With the waning of power of the Gotland Association and the granting of legal status to the Novgorod *Kontor* in 1293, Lübeck had placed itself at the head of the mercantile community. It was Lübeck, too, that initiated the transfer of its mercantile establishments from Bruges to Aardenburg, southern Holland, in 1280 and 1307, as well as the trade blockade against Norway. In 1294 two Dutch towns, Kampen and Zwolle, on the river Ijssel, expressly recognised Lübeck as 'chief and origin of all things'. Trade was regulated and disputes settled in regular Hanseatic assemblies chaired by Lübeck.

From 1358 there are references in the historical sources to an alliance called the *düdesche Hanse* (German Hansa), which was established to safeguard trading advantages. New sea ports and old trading posts joined forces under Lübeck's leadership, in order to represent their mutual interests and facilitate trade and traffic within the Hansa. Although Lübeck took a leading role, its power remained limited. The league of cities lacked a solid structure; the power to make decisions remained with the merchants. The loose alliance had no constitution and the number of its members varied. Hanseatic resolutions – known as *recessi* – were passed in the periodic assemblies of the Hansa. The Hansa's most effective weapons were trade boycotts, and even the blockading of a port or a country, as happened on various occasions. To do this the Hansa needed ships, as they also did to safeguard commerce with their offices in 'foreign cities', for example with the Peterhof in Novgorod, the Stalhof (Steelyard) in London or the Deutsche Brücke (German Bridge) in Bergen.

In foreign cities the members of the Hansa were given secure headquarters and privileges. There the merchants formed a society that was largely able to live according to their own law; sometimes they were even permitted to dispense their own justice and sentence their members to punishment. Another privilege they enjoyed was the exclusive right of Hanseatic ships to sail to the great herring-market in Skåne. In the Hanseatic cities, visiting foreign merchants were obliged to offer their goods for sale under what was called the *Stapelzwang*, or 'stacking enforcement'. This guaranteed that Hanseatic burghers had a prior right of sale over many commodities.

The precise legal form that the Hanseatic League adopted was and is very much in dispute. The Hansa was not so much a fixed alliance of cities as an association of merchants. Up to the middle of the fourteenth century the cities grew into this community by virtue of the fact that their merchants participated in Hanseatic trade. From the middle of that century they drew up formal applications for admission. Admission, withdrawal and exclusion from the Hansa did not imply being granted or refused membership of a league of cities, but only access to privileges under German law. An example may help to explain this. In the course of the hostilities between the Hansa and England in the summer of 1468, English ships were attacked by Danish privateers in the Kattegat. The English held Danzig and the Hansa responsible. King Edward IV arrested the Hanseatic merchants in London and confiscated their goods. His justification was that the Hansa was an association, partnership or community of cities and therefore jointly liable for the actions of its individual members.

On the other hand, the Hansa established in a judicial ruling that it was not a fixed community and did not even possess a joint treasury. It was rather an alliance of cities, each of which pursued its own commercial interests. In this way the Hansa deliberately obfuscated its legal status. The Hansa itself often left unclear the matter of which cities were actually members of the League and which merchants enjoyed its privileges. True, in Lübeck in June 1366 it was resolved that only citizens of the Hanseatic cities should have the freedoms of German merchants, yet soon other merchants, too, were admitted to the *kopmanns recht*, or merchants' rights. Lists have survived from the fifteenth century, which tell us which cities on the North Sea and the Baltic belonged to the Hanseatic League; however, these lists are not always reliable.

THE POWER OF THE HANSA

What was the foundation of Hanseatic power? We have images of fleets of cogs and carracks controlling the Baltic from great port cities like Lübeck. But, important as these maritime trading links were, many of the new cities on the southern Baltic coast grew up at the intersection of land, river and sea routes. Cities of the Hansa included not only sea ports like Bremen, Lübeck, Rostock and Danzig, but also those on navigable rivers, such as Cologne or Dortmund, or towns situated on cross-country trade routes, as Minden was. The truth is that Hanseatic power spanning the North Sea and the Baltic only existed to the extent that it coincided with the interests of the individual cities and their citizenry.

The chief opponents of the Hansa were the evolving territorial states, above all Denmark. In 1360–1 the Danish king Valdemar IV had conquered Skåne, the southernmost province of Sweden, as well as the island of Gotland and its Hanseatic capital, Visby. Therefore Hamburg, Lübeck and the Hanseatic cities of Mecklenburg and Pomerania joined in alliance against Denmark. In April 1362 the cities attacked Copenhagen with a fleet of 52 ships. Not only the fleet but the troops they put ashore were defeated, and the cities were forced to sign an armistice. Then in 1370 renewed hostilities ended in the Treaty of Stralsund – a more favourable outcome for the Hanseatic cities. The Hansa succeeded in obtaining a say in the choice of future Danish kings. Since Danish waters included the important straits of the Great and Little Belt, and the Öresund, Denmark controlled the shipping of goods into and out of the Baltic. This fact, together with the imposition of Danish customs dues, led to frequent disputes, until in 1435 the Hanseatic cities of the southern Baltic were able to free themselves from the *Sundzoll* or Straits Dues. And that was not all. After a further war with Denmark in that year, Lübeck and other Hanseatic cities secured an undertaking from the Danes that Dutch and English ships would be denied access to the Baltic.

The Hanseatic cities also secured risk-free commercial links by means of letters of safe-conduct. Count William II of Holland, for example, granted merchants from Hamburg and Lübeck safe-conduct through his country in return for payment of dues. This enabled the merchants to reach the rich markets of Flanders along Holland's inland waterways, in preference to the dangerous coastal route. In those days there was still a string of connected inland lakes in Holland – the Harlemmer, Leidse and Brasemer meres – so that from the Zuider Zee it was possible to reach Dordrecht and thence Bruges.

The fact that the Hansa obtained such a dominant position was due in part to their excellent ships, but also to their sophisticated trading techniques. For a long time the Hanseatic merchants were alone in being able to handle the exchange of raw materials from the east for manufactured articles from the more advanced west. They also organised the sale throughout Europe of herring caught in the shallow waters off the south coast of Sweden. Seagoing Hanseatic cogs brought in the salt needed for pickling and took away thousands of barrels of pickled herring for the markets of the south. The overseas branches of the Hanseatic League, the *Kontore*, in Novgorod, London, Bergen and Bruges, became important cornerstones of the Hanseatic trading network.

The Hansa also had a lasting influence on the maritime culture of the North Sea and the Baltic, not only through the infrastructure of its ports, but also in the development of maritime law. A system of law grew up governing such matters as loading restrictions, conduct of crews on board and emergencies at sea. The protection of Hanseatic ships by law, especially in foreign ports, was of fundamental importance for a healthy shipping industry.

Later on, the Hanseatic trading zone was subject to the *Waterrecht* or Law of the Water, printed in 1537 and based on older regulations from the Flemish and Dutch trading centres. It was there, in the fourteenth century, that a legal tradition tailored to the needs of merchants and sailors engaged in foreign trade, was laid down in a series of *Waterrechten*. Alongside the maritime legal decisions of the Hanseatic assemblies, and the specific jurisdictions of Lübeck and Hamburg, the *Waterrecht* gained international standing as a source of maritime law. Its 72 articles cover the rights and obligations of a ship's crew and its cargo-owners, and the legal relationship between sea-captains and ship-owners.

The safety of the seaways was crucial to the survival of the Hansa. But the cities did not always sing from the same hymn-sheet. We will see this later on when we turn to the matter of piracy in the Baltic. In order to protect themselves from being boarded by pirates, the ships often sailed in convoy. From 1477 onwards, every fairly large ship had to have 20 armed men aboard, since assaults on the security of shipping could rob individual Hanseatic cities of their life-blood.

DAILY LIFE IN THE HANSEATIC AGE

Historical sources and archaeological finds make it possible to reconstruct a picture of the Hanseatic age, but we know little about how men lived by and on the sea, what their feelings were or what life on board ship was like. We can certainly imagine that at a time when people were far less mobile than today, the sight of many ships in a harbour must have aroused a desire for adventure and distant places. Not a few envious glances were cast toward the rich merchants who were a common sight on the streets of any Hanseatic city. Admission to a *Kontor*, sailing the seas and finally owning a ship were the stuff of dreams. We can imagine that through the mediation of a business partner, a young man full of hopes and dreams might enter the *Kontor* of a wealthy Lübeck merchant, who would have extensive business connections and would be a member of the Council.

In the counting-house

The first few weeks of the young man's career would have been exciting and full of new impressions. The merchant and his clerks would familiarise him with the rules of trade. The clerks recorded all the goods on wax tablets with styluses. The trading-ledger of the Hamburg merchant Vicko von Geldersen (d. 1391) soberly attests to the conduct of Hanseatic merchants. It is true that even in the late fourteenth century some bargains were swiftly concluded with payment of cash and the immediate handing over of goods, yet at the same time there were long-term agreements with outstanding monies or goods due. The parties had these contracts recorded in the *Rathaus* or City Hall in city debt-books, and we have such records in Hamburg from 1288. Nevertheless the procedure was cumbersome. So commercial practice led to the keeping of ledgers of outstanding payments, which would have to stand up in court in the case of disputes. Thus we read in the trading-book of Vicko von Geldersen: 'Gert the rosary-maker, citizen of Lübeck, owes 28 Lübeck marks for a pipe [a medieval measure] of oil, to be paid at Mid-Lent' [on this occasion, 24 March 1381].

The young apprentice would probably have been instructed in how to keep these books. He would learn how to note down the receipt of payments, as well as instalments and the missing of due dates. In Geldersen's trading-book the entries are by different hands, no doubt of clerks and sons of the merchant. The books did not record normal cash transactions. We learn that Geldersen mainly traded in cloth imported from the Netherlands. He also traded with Stade, Lüneberg, Brunswick (Braunschweig) and of course Lübeck. As well as cloth he dealt in timber, iron, foodstuffs, live cattle, pigs and horses, costly spices and luxury goods like silk and gold-inlaid belts. There is one record of the purchase of entire ships, and one of a ship being built to order. The period covered by the book coincides with the Hamburg's economic rise in the years 1381 to 1389. The wealthy merchant was a member of the very grand Flanders Society and from 1387 was a city councillor. In this capacity he took part in the Hanseatic assemblies.

Here was a man who had already 'made it', while our merchant's

In mein Jornal schreib ich all Tag/
Was sich un Gwerb begeben mag/
Mit richtig deutlichem Bescheid/
Welchs zum Bericht dient jederzeit.

Ich soll vertretten den Cassier/
Mit Einund Außgab recht allhier/
Die Cassa ich offt überschlag/
Und den Rest fleissig bey mir trag.

LINGV.

In the *Kontor* or merchant's counting-
house, goods were stored, labelled with
the owner's mark and entered in the
ledgers.

apprentice still gazed out of the window of the *Kontor* at the harbour of Lübeck with its ships and dreamed of foreign lands. However, until then he had to perform other duties, of which he may soon have grown weary. The lead seals attached to the goods had to be examined, and the size of barrels had to be checked with a barrel-measure. The marking of goods with individual symbols indicating ownership, origin and quality played an important part in trade in the Hanseatic era. Thus, for example, from the fourteenth century lead seals were used as a quality-mark for cloth. On some goods little tax-tags were hung, with various markings. In addition there were different kinds of scales and weights, measuring-rods and other equipment, such as special axes for cutting the heads off dried fish in order to save space when stowing them in the hold.

Sometimes the cries of young apprentices might have been heard from the courtyard, when they were being flogged with ropes' ends. There are certainly frequent mentions in eighteenth-century reports of fights between apprentices, clerks and even merchants – it is unlikely to have been any different in the Middle Ages.

On board a Hanseatic ship

It must be true that the varied merchandise from different countries exerted an attraction at first, but soon everything became commonplace, and the goal was to get on board a ship oneself. After some pestering, the young man would have succeeded in getting a berth on the next trading trip – perhaps on a chartered cog in convoy with other vessels – to the markets of Skåne. To board a cog, to sniff the salt air and then watch the crewmen untying the ropes, pushing the ship away from the quay with poles, and unfurling the sail as the vessel glided down the river Trave and out to sea, must have been an exhilarating feeling. Seen from the water, everything looked different and soon the familiar coastline would dwindle to a narrow line on the horizon.

For the seamen this had long since become routine. We can learn something of a sailor's life from the earliest book of Hamburg sea-law, the *Ordelbok* or 'book of judgements', which fixed the terms of chartering in about 1270. A great deal depended on mutual trust. Seamen and ship-owners were the principal parties in the intensive Hanseatic maritime traffic. Since they were carrying costly cargoes on their valuable ships, it is no surprise that from the early thirteenth century onwards the rights and obligations of the seamen, the charterers and the shippers were regulated. These often comprised a typically medieval mixture of cash and profit-sharing.

As we read in the *Ordelbok*, the crews received a weekly *hure* or 'hire'. However, wages paid in advance had to be paid back in full, if the employer could prove that a sailor was unfit for shipboard work owing to constant seasickness or being confined to his bunk for any length of time. In contrast to later times, the seamen, described in the sources as *Schiffskinder* ('ship's children') or simply 'folk', were probably seldom punished, since there are hardly any records of this happening. If there was evidence of a serious crime the most severe penalty a sailor could suffer was to be put ashore on an island. Various regulations served to maintain comradely coexistence on board, the standard of seamanship and the punctual dispatch of the vessel. Anyone caught ashore without leave had to pay a fine of 4 *pfennig*. The seamen were even allowed to carry with them small quantities of merchantable goods for trading on their own account. For many a sailor this would have been the spur to launch them on the ascent from seaman to small-time merchant. This 'right of carriage' had to be paid for if the entire cargo hold was already chartered.

Against the fair legal conditions for the crew weighed the wretched accommodation and a tough service life at sea. Comfort on board was minimal, and only the captain and perhaps the helmsman had their own cabin at the stern, and even a lavatory. At night the crew slept on deck. In a rough sea spray swept over the deck or dripped from the sails. Scarcely an item of clothing stayed dry. Perishable cargoes, such as grain or salt, had to be protected from dampness. When grain was being carried, the hold would be given an extra lining of wood. Liquids such as wine or oil were always carried in barrels.

Returning in our imagination to our Lübeck cog, after several days at sea crossing the Baltic it would have reached the coast of Skåne, the Danish-owned south of Sweden. The young novice merchant's initial sense of adventure had at some point given way to boredom. It was rare to sight another ship on the horizon. And what if they were to encounter the notorious *Vitalienbrüder*, the freebooters of the Baltic? Many sailors had horrific tales to tell. It is true that some Hanseatic cities had links with the *Vitalienbrüder*, but these pirates were always unpredictable. Open-mouthed, our novice merchant listened to the seamen tell of how the freebooters boarded ships, killed any of the crew who tried to fight them off, nailed up the survivors in barrels and locked them below deck, in order to ransom them later. The young merchant shivered; supposing the next sail to appear on the horizon was not a trader?

What use would letters of safe-conduct be then? These documents were supposed to increase security on highways and on sea routes. Under the German (Holy Roman) Empire the right to offer safe-conduct and to levy a fee for this was initially granted by the emperor to local noblemen, until, during the thirteenth century, it was assumed by the nobility as of right. Thus, the Counts of Oldenburg issued letters of safe-conduct to merchants from Osnabrück so that they could visit the St Vitus Market in Oldenburg. In addition to the 'living escort' in the form of armed squads, in the late Middle Ages there appeared the so-called 'dead' escort, or safe-conduct letters promising merchants the protection of the local nobleman. The Hanseatic cities and their merchants possessed many such privileges, which offered political and legal guarantees of their personal safety and that of their goods. At sea these letters were of less use; here, the best form of protection was to sail in convoys, and in dangerous times Hanseatic shipping was guarded by armed 'peace ships'.

In harbour

Soon a new coastline comes into view on the horizon, and suddenly ships appear heading for land from other directions. Gradually the outlines become clearer; trees and buildings become recognisable as our vessel heads for the city harbour in company with foreign ships, and the crew furls our sail on its yardarm. Still under way, the ship glides up to the wooden wharf, and once again the long poles are brought out, to hold the ship clear until the mooring ropes can be secured.

A prayer is offered up in thanks that we have arrived safe and sound in Skåne, along with our cargo. We need fear no protracted and wearisome disputes, for the *Waterrecht* lays down how damage claims between shipmasters and ship-owners are to be settled. It specifies liability and compensation for damages in the case of exceptional events during the voyage, such as collisions, the loss of cargo overboard during a storm or the mortgaging of the ship and its cargo in a foreign country.

The different ships lying closely packed in harbour were similarly built, but had their individual characteristics. Some of them were *Umlandfahrer*, the name given to merchants and their ships whose voyages took them round the northern tip of Jutland and into the North Sea. Like the Lübeck ships, these too had to pay Skåne dues to the Danish king.

After the ship had moored, the merchant or his clerks would come on board. The cargo stored in barrels was brought ashore and taken to the *Kontor*. Heavy goods were lifted out of the ship with the aid of a block-and-tackle, a yard-arm serving as a derrick, or with a heavy crane powered by a treadmill, then lowered onto the wharf or into a lighter. Fixed tariffs regulated the wage the crane-men or porters could demand. Where the cargo was not unloaded directly onto the wharf, lighters would take the goods ashore from ships anchored in the roadstead.

A painting from a Flemish Book of
Hours shows a crane in operation in
the Hanseatic city of Bruges.

Cranes driven by treadmills made it possible to lift heavy goods. This replica of a medieval crane can be seen in Bruges.

Trade was conducted in Low German, a tongue closer to Dutch than modern *Hochdeutsch*. But other languages were heard, which the Lübeckers would not have understood. Fresh goods were brought on board from the *Kontor* and stowed in the spacious hold of the cog. There was time enough to look around the foreign city and to stroll into one of the inns that could be found near the harbour. Here they would meet other merchants, seamen and craftsmen, as well as the usual riff-raff who hung around on the waterfront.

Money and power

This first voyage would doubtless be followed by others. On each one the raw clerk would learn more, and sooner or later would become a merchant himself. Perhaps with help from a wealthy relative he would succeed in opening his own *Kontor* to conduct overseas trade. At first he would probably have to borrow money to rent a counting-house. Perhaps a good marriage would help him to progress further up the social ladder. Now he was very much the merchant, who no longer went to sea himself but controlled his commerce from his own *Kontor*, calculating and reflecting on what goods he would buy and sell, and at what prices. Many of these decisions he would not make alone but in conjunction with other merchants in the Hansa. The association offered protection, but were its members really free? It is true that they owned their own counting-houses, but the adventure of sail, of seeking out foreign markets and cities, had now given place to mere book-keeping.

HANSEATIC CITIES ON THE BALTIC

As the Hansa emerged in the form of an exclusive association of merchants, the merchants' quarters in the cities also began to change – something we have chiefly learned from archaeological excavations in Lübeck.

From the time when merchants began to conduct their business from *Kontoren* in their home cities, the small wooden structures near the waterfront gave way to large brick houses with cellars and storage lofts. These were both the residences and the business headquarters of the merchants. Barter had been replaced by book-keeping, and by transactions on credit or commission. Thus self-governing boroughs, responsible for their own defence, grew up. This new form of city, with its own harbour, became in the late thirteenth century, the *civitas maritima*.

Such 'sea-cities' came to typify the Hanseatic era. The harbour had its own fortifications, and nearby were a rectangular marketplace with a market church (*ecclesia forensis*) and city hall, usually built in red brick in the Gothic style. The growth in commerce and in the size of ships required larger wharves and warehouses. Merchants and artisans found room and protection for their activities within the city's fortified walls. The market and the harbour formed the two economic pillars of these cities, while the *Rathaus* or city hall, and the church, showed who wielded power over the life of the citizens. Some of these new sea ports were founded from scratch by settlers or local noblemen, while others were Wendish (Slav) towns, which had been adapted to the demands of expanding maritime activity. This is clearly demonstrated by the growth of Lübeck, providing the pattern for cities founded on the southern Baltic coast, such as Wismar, Rostock, Stralsund and Greifswald.

Lübeck

Count Adolf II of Schauenburg had acquired eastern Holstein from the Slavs as a means of consolidating his power. At the same time he moved the trading post of Old Lübeck upstream to the island of Bucu, lying between the Trave and Wakenitz rivers. The hill on the island, which was already settled by Slavs, offered a more protected site for a trading post than Old Lübeck

Even on the side facing the harbour, the medieval Hanseatic cities were fortified with walls and gates. This 1498 painting by Hans Memling depicts the arrival of St Ursula in Cologne, which in the fifteenth century was an important Hanseatic city.

had done. The current in the Trave was not so strong as to cause the ships to break loose from their moorings, yet the water was deep enough to give good access to and from the Baltic.

These good communications enabled the new trading settlement on the island of Bucu to grow rapidly and become a dangerous rival to Bardowic, a trading town that owed allegiance to the Saxon duke, Heinrich the Lion. Initially, the duke forbade his vassal, Count Adolf, to hold any more markets for foreign goods in Lübeck. This was as great a disaster for the new town as was the devastating fire that swept through it at about the same time. The inhabitants now asked Duke Heinrich to found *another* new town, but Count Adolf rejected the new site and in time Duke Heinrich relented, becoming an important champion of Lübeck's development. The citizens' committee of Lübeck, which had existed since 1143, was made up of a close-knit group of merchants who traded overseas. At that time they had already formed a guild but not a council with independent powers. Duke Heinrich's steward still had the last word in the town. This situation continued until Duke Heinrich granted Lübeck a city charter in 1159.

Lübeck retained its medieval appearance well into the modern era, as this seventeenth-century engraving shows.

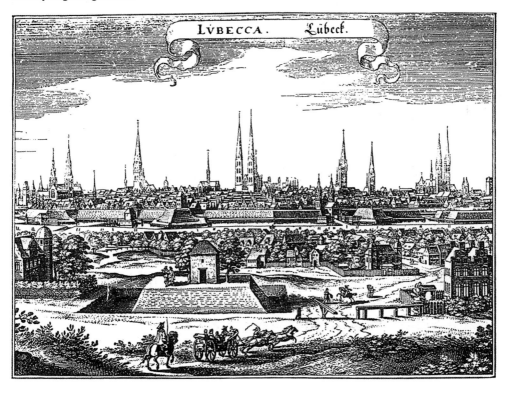

The wealth and influence of the merchants was displayed in the city's buildings. Around the old riverside market great trading houses sprang up, to provide permanent accommodation and offices for the merchants. These simple, wooden-floored halls were soon enlarged on either side. Then, from around 1180, the owner's private apartments were added. From about 1268, multi-storied brick houses began to appear, which were now status symbols of the mercantile class. These grand houses, built around a large central hall and heated by stoves, offered not only greater comfort and protection against fire, but also increased storage capacity for goods in mass quantities. In the late Middle Ages the gabled frontages already made up the prestigious townscape that typifies Lübeck to this day. On the small strip of land between the quays and the city walls, it was no longer possible to stack goods, as it had been in the old riverside market. The freight was carried through the gates into the city and stored in the *Kontoren* or sold in the central market. Adjoining the merchants' quarter on the north side of the city was the artisans' quarter. Archaeological excavations show that between 1217 and 1240 there was a genuine building boom, which cannot be explained except by the city's headlong economic, demographic and political expansion.

In 1226 Lübeck was one of the first cities in Germany to succeed in wresting power from its feudal landowner and placing itself under the direct rule of the Emperor. The city became a *freie Reichstadt*, or free imperial city, and was largely self-governing. Its constitution was shaped ever more strongly by the needs of the merchants. Lübeck's commercial and maritime law was later adopted by many newly founded cities in the Baltic region, which had the advantage of giving the merchants greater legal security in their trade from city to city: wherever Lübeck's law prevailed, there were registers of debt and property ownership, and elaborate laws governing bills of exchange and bankruptcy. The road from a unified legal system to a federation of cities was not a long one.

Mecklenburg, Pomerania and the Baltic lands

As in Lübeck, there now arose in other coastal regions around the Baltic the typical walled sea ports with docks and *Kontoren*. If we look at the network of cities in the entire Baltic region, we find that it includes most of the cities from Schleswig-Holstein eastwards as far as East Prussia. In the areas of German eastward colonisation – Mecklenburg, Pomerania and the territories of the Teutonic Knights – the settlement continued to become denser into the thirteenth and fourteenth centuries. The first sea ports that grew up east of Lübeck were mostly small, at best medium-sized towns. In

The *Minnesänger* (minstrel) Friedrich von Hausen
is usually depicted on a ship. It is possible that
people were thinking of his namesake, who was
Bishop of Kulm on the Baltic around 1276. The
fur hood worn by Friedrich in the picture
suggests northern climes.

some cases they had been preceded by a trading post. Since the merchants regarded St Nicholas as their patron saint, parish churches bearing his name to this day are often built on the sites of older merchant churches.

The further expansion of towns and cities like Wismar, Rostock, Stralsund, Danzig, Riga and Tallinn (then known by its mainly German inhabitants as Reval) took place in step with their prospering commerce. The merchants in these ports organised a large part of the trade in bulk goods in the Baltic region. Here deep-sea fishing and overseas trade joined in the search for markets. They had access to salt from Lüneburg and from salt-pans near Rostock. This meant that foodstuffs, especially herrings, could be preserved and traded.

As early as the mid-twelfth century the harbour of Wismar was already being used by the Danes. At that time the town served as the port for Mecklenburg, the stronghold and population centre of the Obodrites, as well as for Schwerin, the seat of the bishopric. Wismar had grown out of the merging of three settlements, as the entrepôt between sea-borne and inland trade. In 1266, Wismar's development was boosted by the introduction of Lübeck law, which cemented the predominance of the city council. The burghers' city was surrounded by a wall, which at the same time separated it from the castle of the feudal lord. This was a visible expression of the independence of the burghers from the prince.

As in Wismar, in Slavic times a trading settlement grew up beside the river Warnow, though this was destroyed by the Danish king, Valdemar I, in 1160. Only a short time later, the Prince of Rostock opened a market and thus laid the foundation-stone for yet another maritime trading city: Rostock. Similarly, Stralsund became an important centre for the Principality of Rügen, and attracted the herring-fleets that fished off the coast of the island of Rügen. Although a connection to the sea was of special importance, mooring-places and harbours chiefly grew up were there were also good links with the hinterland that was becoming more densely populated. The ideal position was where a major river flowed into the sea; this is demonstrated by the growth of the Hanseatic city of Danzig (now Gdansk in Poland).

Danzig was not a new foundation in the Middle Ages, for in Slavic times there was already an important fortress and settlement on the island where the river Vistula divides into two before flowing into the Baltic. In the twelfth century the first German merchants moved to the Vistula estuary and soon settled there. They formed their own association under German law.

Close to the market a church was built in 1185–90, dedicated to St Nicholas, the patron saint of seafarers. The independent German *civitas*, existing alongside the Slav settlement, reached its zenith around 1300.

The rise of German Baltic trade was also favoured by the fact that the Crusader movement was flaring up again in Europe. In the Baltic region there was a drive to Christianise the Livonians, Letts (Latvians), Courlanders and Estonians. In 1201 Riga was founded as an important stronghold on the river Daugava, and its rise as a centre of foreign trade was promoted by Lübeck. The trading contacts of the German overseas merchants in the Baltic even extended as far as Holland and England.

HANSEATIC CITIES ON THE NORTH SEA

After the Baltic, the North Sea was the Hansa's second largest maritime trading area. From Dorestad on the Lower Rhine extensive sea routes had developed from around AD 700. In the High Middle Ages Dorestad was supplanted by the Friesian ports of Staveren and Groningen, by Deventer on the navigable Ijssel, Tiel on the Waal and Utrecht, which in the eleventh century became the principal entrepôt between the North Sea and the Baltic. In the twelfth century the merchants who met in Utrecht's four great annual markets were mainly from foreign countries. But since, even in the thirteenth century, the Netherlanders had scarcely any commercial expertise, merchants from Bremen, Hamburg and Lübeck obtained letters of safe-conduct for their journeys to Utrecht in the County of Holland and Zeeland. Yet a more important destination for the travellers was the coast of Flanders with its many cities, especially Bruges. However, the voyages of the Hanseatic ships also took them into the Norwegian Sea and beyond, seeking the sulphur, whale-oil, fish and wool that Iceland could provide.

Bremen and Hamburg

Among the entrepôts for North Sea trade that grew in importance were the Hanseatic cities of north-west Germany, Bremen and Hamburg. Bremen had grown up on the west bank of the river Weser, at an important crossing point where the river with its marshy lowlands reached a long chain of dunes. The only road across the dunes ran from north-west to south-east, then through the boggy area of the Bremen basin. Up to this point the ships could sail in and out on the tides.

We first hear of Bremen, or *Bremum* as it was originally named, in the 'Life of St Willehad', in connection with the Saxon uprising against the Franks in 782. The town's economic and political development was boosted by the move there of the episcopal seat in 845, after Hamburg had been laid waste in a Viking attack. As early as 888 Bremen was granted the right to mint coins, hold markets and levy tolls, and in 1189 the council of Bremen freed the city from the rule of the bishops. The relationship with the increasingly powerful Hansa was not without conflict, since the citizens of Bremen were indulging in piracy, and even after Bremen's admission to the Hansa it continued to condone the sale of stolen goods in their market. Around 1400, after a period of crisis and disputes, the city's economic situation improved, as is shown by the layout of the centre with its city hall and market.

Like Bremen, Hamburg also grew up at an important river crossing. At the point where the river Alster flowed into the Elbe, a Saxon settlement had existed before the Franks fortified the town and made it their stronghold on the northern boundary of their sphere of influence. The early inhabitants of Hamburg had to resist various attacks by Vikings and Slavs. From the late twelfth century the city extended beyond its old boundaries. A place whose chief significance had owed more to the pattern of overland trade routes, now developed into a port whose ships plied the medieval seas. They were so successful that in 1188 Hamburg copied Lübeck in laying out a modern port. This development took place over a span of two centuries and can still be traced today in the city's waterfront district.

Even during the ninth century, at the foot of the Hammaburg fortress, merchants' plots with blocks of wooden houses stretched for at least a hundred yards parallel with the Elbe, in the area of today's Reichsstrassenfleet. From 1147 the overseas trade market in the west of the city grew rapidly as the *Ufermarkt* ('riverside market'). Over several centuries the bank was reinforced and probably a series of jetties was built at an early stage. Then in 1157 the construction of quays and wharves began. Numerous remains of nails and rivets in excavations indicate that ships were built and repaired here. Many of these ships would have sailed to Gotland, the most important entrepôt for goods from the east, or to the herring-markets of Skåne, in southern Sweden. Here merchants from England and the Netherlands met those from the Baltic. By about 1500, Hamburg had a population of some 15,000, and together with Bremen it grew during the sixteenth century to become a strong competitor to the Baltic ports. With the decline of the Hansa, Hamburg exploited its location, which gave it maritime links to the whole world. It even attracted Lübeck's Baltic trade.

There were a number of riverside fortresses securing the course of the Elbe between Hamburg and the sea. Generally these were simple, multi-storeyed stone towers such as those at Neuwerk and Ritzebüttel near Cuxhaven. On the island of Neuwerk in the Elbe estuary a stone tower offered both security and navigational guidance to shipping. From here the estuary could be monitored – although in the Middle Ages it was not impregnable, as numerous attacks by peasants from south-western Holstein were to prove. True, Hamburg had agreements with the parishes of that district, but what use were they when the peasants of the 'Süderstrand' simply stripped the Hanseatic cogs bare of their rich cargoes! These attacks, like the forts intended to deter them, show how important the sea routes had become.

Dithmarschen

In relation to the Hansa and its sea-borne trade, the coastal region of Dithmarschen occupied a special position. It had no large port, yet its yeoman farmers played an important part in commerce. No prince, nor even the Bishop of Bremen, was able to impose his authority on this inaccessible territory, bounded on its landward side by treacherous bogs. Instead, until 1447, Dithmarschen was a confederation of parishes, governed by council assemblies, called *Kollegien,* in which the ruling class made decisions about the building of dykes, highway matters, local defence and trade. The importance of sea-borne trade to Dithmarschen is shown by the fact that for a whole century the Hanseatic assemblies debated over whether it should be admitted to their councils. The question was never settled, but in 1559 the Danish king and the Duke of Holstein joined forces to subdue the Dithmarschers and divide the territory between them. It was the end of independence for a community that had been only nominally subordinate to the bishopric of Bremen.

Flanders and Bruges

In the eleventh and twelfth centuries the Flemish textile weaving enjoyed an unparalleled boom, and as early as the twelfth century Flemish cloth was being sold from the Mediterranean to the Baltic. Bruges was one of the centres of this industrialised production of cloth. True, there were towns in Flanders that produced more cloth than it did, but Bruges had the priceless advantage of being accessible from the North Sea, via the river Zwin. Following a storm-surge in 1134 the navigable channel of the Zwin became so deep that seagoing vessels could sail inland from the North Sea. Admittedly, the river did not reach the city itself; the last few miles were completed by the canalisation of a stream, making it navigable by small vessels called *schuten*. Around 1435, a Spanish nobleman named Pero Tafur wrote that on some days no fewer than 700 *schuten* left Bruges. As Bruges grew to be the international marketplace of the Middle Ages, the Flemish merchants withdrew from active participation in foreign trade and took their profit as brokers. However, this made them dependent on good access for shipping, and when the Zwin silted up and the city lost its connection to the sea, Bruges's decline began.

In Hanseatic cities life was centred on the harbour.
This woodcut depicts the port of Antwerp c. 1515.

Antwerp, on the western Scheldt, could easily be reached from the sea and replaced Bruges as the port for Flanders. It is this fact that we must thank for the almost perfect preservation of Bruges as a medieval city.

London

Quite a number of the English ships sailing into Antwerp were from London. Following the marauding raids by the Vikings, who found that the Thames estuary gave them a gateway to southern England, London had been more strongly fortified, and commerce retreated behind the city walls. A port grew up on the Thames that was regularly visited by merchants from Flanders, Normandy, the Ile de France and the towns of the Meuse valley. However, the greatest privileges were those enjoyed by the guild of Rhenish merchants, which later became the London Hansa.

It appears that, around the year 1000, the foreign merchants settled a little way downstream from London Bridge. According to a customs document drawn up some time between 991 and 1002, London Bridge was at that time the place were small fishing-boats were beached. Not until after 1000 did the building of quays and wharves begin. In the reign of Edward the Confessor (1048–66) there is mention of a 'wharf' in London. Ulf, the portreeve of London, gave the port and its associated land to Westminster Abbey, thereby acquiring the right to load and unload goods free of royal tolls.

At the beginning of the twelfth century foreign vessels usually moored at wharfs above London Bridge. The wine trade was concentrated in a district later called the Vintry. Archaeological finds in this district show that there

London was one of the foremost foreign strongholds of the Hanseatic League.

Detail of an early illustrative map of London. The *Stalhof* (Steelyard) occupies more or less the central block.

were intensive contacts with the Rhineland. In 1175 merchants from Cologne set up business in London, acquiring a building on the riverside, east of Dowgate – the Guildhall. The merchants could move freely on the waterfront and conduct their trade around the ships and the warehouses. Along the Roman wall numerous wooden wharves banked with earth were built on a 17-metre-wide waterfront. This meant that the embankment became ever wider. In 1301 the bank of the Thames was already 91 m south of Thames Street. Narrow alleys now led through a densely built-up area to the river. Because of the fast tidal stream, quays extending further into the river had to be built of stone.

With its increasing political importance in the Middle Ages, London grew to be the second-largest city in northern Europe after Paris. Its population rose to over 80,000, and more and more businesses were concentrated there. Written sources from 1125 and later mention the large number of German merchants and their involvement in grain trade. Other commodities traded were fish, wine and products from the Baltic region. Around 1250 the German community in London increased sharply in size. In 1260 Henry III, at the request of his brother, the king of Germany, granted the merchants of the German (Holy Roman) Empire their own headquarters in London, known as the *Gildehall teutonicorum*. It was the same building that had earlier been confirmed as the property of the merchants of Cologne. The merchants of Hamburg and Lübeck also established their own *Hansa* in London, which they called the *Stalhof* (Steelyard).

THE DECLINE OF THE HANSEATIC LEAGUE

Despite the weakness of its institutions and its internal disunity, the Hanseatic League dominated maritime commerce in the North Sea and the Baltic for four centuries. However, as the Nordic nations gained in strength and confidence the Hansa was confronted by opponents who in the long run proved too powerful to oppose.

With the discovery of new continents and sea routes and the growth of new nation-states, the pattern of economic and political forces had shifted to the disadvantage of the Hanseatic League. Critically, the Atlantic and trading links with the Americas became more important than the North Sea and the Baltic. As an organisation, the Hansa was not well-suited to the new economic and political circumstances. It even had to close down its overseas *Kontore*, the Peterhof in Novgorod in 1494 and London's Stalhof in 1598. When the last Hanseatic assembly met in Lübeck in 1699, there were several attempts to organise the Hansa as a federation of cities, but all failed. What remained was the alliance between the cities of Hamburg, Bremen and Lübeck, which had been signed in 1630.

THE *VITALIENBRÜDER*: PRIVATEERS OF THE BALTIC[1]

The story of the *Vitalienbrüder* begins in 1380 with a commonplace brawl in a beer-cellar in the city of Wismar. The city's *Liber proscriptorum*, which was kept from 1353 to 1429, records a quarrel between two ruffians. This book, containing the earliest court records of Wismar, lists numerous committals, complaints, penalties and pardons. The entry concerning this affray would be unremarkable, had not one of the assailants been a man identified as 'Nicolao Stortebeker'. There is some evidence that this was in fact the Klaus Störtebeker who became a legend as the most famous of the band of privateers known as the *Vitalienbrüder*. Wismar was one of the cities they used as a base, for in the disputes between Mecklenburg and Denmark over Baltic supremacy, the *Vitalienbrüder* took the side of the dukes of Mecklenburg.

In Denmark, the widowed Margarete was engaged in a struggle for power following the death of her father, King Valdemar IV. In an attempt to seize the Danish throne, Duke Albrecht of Mecklenburg, who was also king of Sweden from 1383 to 1389, tried to force a marriage with her. However, in 1387 the Danish National Council declared Margarete queen regnant of Denmark (and Norway), and she chose another husband in preference to Albrecht, so that she could rule in her own right. The ducal house of Mecklenburg was now unable to equip a navy of its own, but instead sought allies among the commercial ship-owners in what became known as the *Kaperkrieg*, or Privateers' War, against Denmark. It was the first time in the history of Nordic hostilities that use had been made of pirates. The Chronicle of Lübeck, by the scribe Detmar, gives this account:

> *In the same year, when the ships from Rostock and Wismar were setting sail for Stockholm under Duke Johann, the men from Rostock und Wismar made a proclamation that whosoever wished to try his luck as a freebooter at his own expense, in order to harm the realms of Denmark and Norway, should assemble in the cities of Rostock and Wismar, to be given 'letters-of-marque' [official permission to commit piracy], which gave them leave freely to share out, exchange and sell the plundered goods. The Prince ordered that the same be proclaimed, and that the ports of Ribnitz and Golwitz should be opened for all those who wished to harm those aforenamed realms.*

---

[1] During the Hundred Years' war the people who provisioned the army were called *vitailleurs*. In 1394, when Mecklenburg was at war with Denmark, the Dukes of Mecklenburg hired pirates (known as *Vitalienbrüder*) whose job was to maintain a supply of food for the city of Stockholm, under siege by the Danes.

In this way, the nobility of Mecklenburg entered into a compact with bands of roving and unorganised pirates, and the boundaries with mercenary service became blurred. Thus it is hardly surprising that people at this time had difficulty in categorising the phenomenon of piracy. Throughout the sources from this period, the pirates are described as *sevore* ('sea-robbers'). The poverty of some of the minor aristocracy may well have encouraged them to support or indeed join the pirates, in the hope of sharing some of their booty, as some did with the highwaymen of the countryside.

Thus, with the opening of the Mecklenburg ports to all 'who wished to harm the Nordic realms', the Privateers' War began. All manner of criminals, journeymen, ruffians and disaffected peasantry and townspeople foregathered in the port cities and, since they received no regular pay, became what were known as *Vitalienbrüder*, who from now on survived on the prospect of obtaining wealth through plunder.

The *Vitalienbrüder* became a new and unpredictable power, no longer beholden to anyone. In the written sources, we not only find the name '*Vitalienbrüder*', but also '*Likedeeler*' ('equal sharers'). Yet the risks the pirates took were not small. For the Mecklenburg letters-of-marque (of which unfortunately no examples survive) did not exempt the *Vitalienbrüder* from severe punishment if they were taken prisoner. Thus we read in one of the Hanseatic *recessi*:

> It came to pass, however, in this year [1391] that a number of these Vitalienbrüder *attacked a ship from Stralsund and attempted to take it by force, even though they heard and saw that its crew were not Danes but Germans. But the men on the Stralsund ship defended themselves and overcame the* Vitalienbrüder *and captured more than a hundred... They took barrels, of which they had many on board, struck the bottoms out of them, and made a hole in the top large enough to hold a man by the neck. Then they stuffed the* Vitalienbrüder *into the barrels, one after the other, so that their heads stuck out of the top. Then they nailed the bottoms shut again. They stacked up the barrels as one is accustomed to do, but with the men in them, and brought them to Stralsund. The* Vitalienbrüder *remained in the barrels until they were taken in carts to the place where they were to be beheaded. The Stralsunders had learnt this method of dealing with prisoners from the* Vitalienbrüder *themselves, who had mistreated and martyred many a poor Dane in just the same way.*
>
> Hanseatic Recessi, *I, 4*

The hostilities between the non-Mecklenburg cities of the Hanseatic League and the *Vitalienbrüder* were conducted on both sides with implacable harshness. However, to begin with, there were no combined Hanseatic operations; rather, the alliance of cities attempted to remain neutral in the early phases of the conflict between Denmark and Mecklenburg, and not to become involved in a costly war at sea. The Hansa even reacted in a conciliatory manner to complaints from Prussian cities about the pirates of Mecklenburg.

It was now that Mecklenburg's Hanseatic cities, Rostock and Wismar, ought really to have associated themselves with the League's operations against the pirates. It is true that the Hansa granted these cities a certain degree of privileged status, but in May 1377, it issued a decree banning the purchase of goods obtained through piracy. However, Rostock and Wismar persisted in their support for Mecklenburg and its pirates. As already explained, these pirates were not paid mercenaries, but acted on their own account, attacking Hanseatic as well as Danish vessels. Unsurprisingly, it was soon realised that these privateers were causing enormous harm to shipping. Early in 1378, therefore, the Hanseatic assembly decided to have armed cogs – known as peace-ships – fitted out by Lübeck, Stralsund and Greifswald. But in 1380 these operations were brought to an end owing to the high costs. Furthermore, for a short time there was peace with Denmark, as Duke Albrecht of Mecklenburg had died. Thus the Hanseatic ships were left without the protection they needed, and many cogs were attacked by pirates. Things could not go on like thus. On 27 January an

Cogs being deployed in war at sea in the early thirteenth century.

assembly of delegates from Lübeck, Rostock, Stralsund and Wismar agreed to fit out more warships. Four large vessels, probably cogs, and ten small, manoeuvrable, shallow-draught boats called *Schniggen* all set sail, fully crewed and provisioned. The privateers, who were no longer able to operate from Mecklenburg ports, were given temporary asylum by Danish noblemen. On 15 September 1381, Denmark did succeed in brokering a peace-treaty with the pirates, but this did not hold for long. In the period that followed, the Danish queen, Margarete, also began to take action against the pirates. The Hansa returned to the queen her four fortresses on the Öresund strait and in exchange she granted the Hansa trading privileges in Denmark. The burgomaster of Stralsund, Wulfan, entrusted the Hanseatic League with the task of pacifying the Baltic.

Yet this peace in the Baltic remained no more than a brief interlude, since in 1390 Mecklenburg intervened in the hostilities between Denmark and Sweden. Again there was an attempt to weaken the Danish opposition through waging a privateer war against its shipping. In that same year came the first complaints about ships being attacked. The port of Visby on Gotland, which had been under Danish rule since 1361, stated in a letter to the Hanseatic League, that 'captains from Rostock and Wismar have captured ships owned by our citizens'.

In the late summer of 1392 the situation in the Baltic became so acute that shipping could only proceed in convoy to have any hope of safety. Two unescorted ships from Elbing were attacked by the *Vitalienbrüder* off the island of Bornholm, and one of them had the misfortune, after being released, to fall into Danish hands. On 22 April 1393 the *Vitalienbrüder* even attacked Bergen in Norway. However, the leaders of this operation were not the usual captains, but probably members of the highest aristocracy of Mecklenburg. In a chronicle from the city of Lübeck (the so-called Rufus Chronicle) we read:

> *In the same year... the* Vitalienbrüder *from Rostock and Wismar sailed to Norway and maltreated the merchants at Bergen; they took many valuables of gold and silver and costly garments, household goods and even fish. With this great treasure they then sailed unhindered back to Rostock and sold it among the citizenry.*

Between 1391 and 1395 many *Vitalienbrüder* were under the command of Mecklenburg noblemen and were deployed alongside regular Mecklenburg troops; the distinction between these two groups was doubtless rather fluid. In the written sources for this period we read about a whole series of *capitanei* and *fratres vitualium*, in other words captains and *Vitalienbrüder*. However, Klaus Störtebeker and Godeke Michels do not yet appear by name. The majority of *Vitalien* captains in the period from 1392 to 1394 clearly came from Mecklenburg's lesser noble families. But among the captains that we know about there was at least one Danish aristocrat and two mendicant monks from Visby. During the Mecklenburg–Danish war, between 1391 and 1394, the activities of these privateers led to an almost complete shutdown of Hanseatic shipping in the Baltic.

The chronicler Reimar Kock noted for the year 1393 that 'the *Vitalienbrüder* had mastery of the sea and caused harm to every ship, wherefore at Lübeck the entire fleet remained idle, which was no little loss to the townspeople'. The prices of grain and fish rose. The herring-catch dropped to a quarter or one-fifth of its former level. This too shows how important the smooth functioning of mercantile shipping was to the cities. The chronicler Detmar of Lübeck remarked that the '*Vitalienbrüder* robbed both friend and foe alike, so that the trade with Skåne languished for all of three years. Therefore in that year herring was much dearer.' The Lübeck merchants shipped salt from the salt-pans of Lüneburg to Skåne, where it was used to preserve the herring. This trade came to a standstill. This not only affected Lübeck but also Denmark, since the customs revenue, which Queen Margarete would normally have levied, ceased to be collected. A peaceful settlement had to be reached, and Lübeck attempted to mediate between Denmark and Mecklenburg. In order to secure a stronger negotiating position, Margarete tried to capture Stockholm, but in 1394 the princes of Mecklenburg sent a fleet in a support of the Swedes, thus thwarting the plan of the Danish queen.

Vessels from Wismar formed part of this fleet, and Klaus Störtebeker and Godeke Michels may well have been on board, though written historical sources do not confirm this. However, since the two men are named for the first time as captains of the *Vitalienbrüder,* they could have won their spurs in this operation. Thus Störtebeker and Michels belong to a period between 1391 and 1395 when the *Vitalienbrüder* again began to operate in an increasingly autonomous manner, while other regular troops were brought in as reinforcements by the Dukes of Mecklenburg. On the other hand, for the *Vitalienbrüder* sailing under an independent flag, their only connection with the local Mecklenburg rulers was the fact that they could use their harbours.

Since a peace treaty was still not in sight, Lübeck and its allied Hanseatic cities now resolved to get rid of the pirate problem once and for all, by

possit vide
frante vo m
orbs cuisdem
tens m sum
mali bn vide
signu illuo·
oailus coisus
pede mali m
orct vide su
q̃ quicst m
mitate· qua
pinquior est
noin pede q̃ m
sumitate fru
plmeas duct
ab vt̃q̃ad sut
Et mulla ab
ius rci tu est
tumor ag· E

Bearings are taken on a landmark
from the crows-nest and from the
ship's deck.

raising a fleet of 36 cogs and four Rhine-ships (small, manoeuvrable freighters) with 3,500 men under arms. Each cog was to have a *schute* and a *schnigge* in attendance. For those days this was a vast fleet. Unfortunately it remained no more than a plan, since the Prussian cities of the Hansa repeatedly withdrew their contributions. Negotiations over peace in the Baltic continued to drag on. To make matters worse, the island of Gotland, then in the possession of the Danish queen, was captured by the captain of Stockholm, Albrecht von Pecatel, with a large contingent of *Vitalienbrüder*. This improved the strategic position of Mecklenburg, an ally in the peace negotiations.

These now began on 20 May 1395, in two Skåne towns, Falsterbro and Skanör, between the Hanseatic League, the Teutonic Knights, Queen Margarete and Mecklenburg. One of the terms of the treaty concluded was that the *Vitalienbrüder* had to leave the Baltic by 25 July 1395, since their unfettered power had become a danger to all. Another reason was that the pirates had established fortified bases on the Gulf of Bothnia and the Gulf of Finland, from where they could harass the sea routes of the eastern Baltic.

The new treaty made things very difficult for the *Vitalienbrüder*, since they were liable to lose their coastal bases. They now split up into small groups, and a number of them still tried to hold on to their position in the Baltic. Because the treaty had not fully returned Gotland to Queen Margarete, the Danish–Mecklenburg conflict smouldered on, and the *Vitalienbrüder* who had remained on Gotland began to build up its capital, Visby, as their maritime stronghold. The plunder of shipping was of course their livelihood. A large number of their ships lay at anchor in Stockholm, while a few sailed for Finland, which meant that they still posed a risk to merchant shipping. What is more, the Mecklenburg nobility, for so long allied with the privateers, were gradually losing their grip on the situation in Gotland. From their base in Visby, the *Vitalienbrüder* began an extensive privateering campaign against all merchant shipping in the Baltic. However, in doing so the pirates now alienated all the major powers.

In the end it was the High Master of the Teutonic Knights, Konrad von Jungingen, who made preparations for an invasion of Gotland. On 17 March 1398, a fleet of 84 vessels with 4,000 men in armour and 400 horses, left the mouth of the Vistula, and after a voyage of four days reached Gotland. In the ensuing siege of the *Vitalienbrüder*, the superiority of the Teutonic troops became clear, and they captured the city. Most of the pirates were slaughtered. According to historical records, three other 'pirate castles' on the island were burnt down. A good five weeks after setting forth, the Teutonic fleet sailed into the Vistula again. The power of the *Vitalienbrüder*, who, between 1395 and 1398, had inflicted such damage on merchant shipping in the Baltic, was broken.

Gotland was now lost to the *Vitalienbrüder*, they no longer controlled any ports, and, just as important, had nowhere to sell their booty; so the last of them were forced to leave the Baltic. The majority sailed into the North Sea.

THE *VITALIENBRÜDER* IN THE NORTH SEA

For the *Vitalienbrüder*, the North Sea with its trade routes to England had always been just as attractive a hunting-ground as the Baltic. We know that these privateers were plundering North Sea shipping as early as 1395. Furthermore, the political situation in the North Sea countries was very favourable to those bent on seizing and selling booty. The coast of eastern Friesland, with its extensive marshes, was not under the domination of any single feudal landlord, but was divided into different rural parishes, over which local *hovetlinge*, or chieftains, exercised power.

These chieftains originally came from rich and powerful families. They fought among themselves and often engaged in feuds with the Counts of Holland and Oldenburg as well. In the late fourteenth century, the *Vitalienbrüder* could usefully be deployed in these incessant campaigns, since they were independent, owned their own ships, were battle-hardened and cost little, as they took booty in lieu of pay. In return, the Friesian chieftains could offer the pirates what they most needed: secure harbours, hideouts and markets for plundered goods. The most important of those who harboured the pirates were Edo Wiemken, Keno tom Brok, Hisko of Emden and the Cirksena family in the towns of Norden and Greetsiel. However, the chieftains, like the Mecklenburg princes before them, were soon to find out that the *Vitalienbrüder* were far from easy to control. What is more, the *Vitalienbrüder* brought the Friesian chieftains into still greater conflict with external forces. The sharp increase of piracy in the southern North Sea also damaged Hanseatic shipping and particularly affected Hamburg and Bremen with their exports to the west.

Among the *Vitalienbrüder* who probably moved into the North Sea in 1398 were Klaus Störtebeker and Godeke Michels. The way in which the pirates went about their work is described in an account from the Hanseatic *Kontor* in Bruges:

The Vitalienbrüder, *to whom Widzel tom Brok [one of the Friesian chieftains] had given domicile in Friesland, recently took over a ship*

in Norway laden with beer from Wismar, whose master was one Egghert Schoeff of Danzig. In this ship the same Vitalienbrüder sailed from Norway past the Zwin estuary [the river linking Bruges with the North Sea] into the Straits of Calais [i.e. of Dover] and there they captured 14 or 15 ships laden with all manner of goods... At the same time they also captured a ship which came from England and was bound for the Zwin. In this vessel the merchants of our law [i.e. Hanseatic] lost large quantities of gold and of cloth, and the pirates took these merchants with them to Friesland, as we have heard. And after they had taken all the ships they wanted, they then sold back to the said ship-master Egghert Schoeff his ship for a sum of money, for which he was held hostage, so that he could only claim the money from Widzel tom Brok in Friesland. The ship-master Egghert Schoeff also informed us that the Vitalienbrüder had ordered him to tell us that they were God's friends and foes of all the world, except those from Hamburg and Bremen, to whom they wished to do no harm, since they were allowed to come and go there whenever they pleased.
Hanseatic Recessi, I, 4

We may be sure that Hamburg and Bremen were not as well disposed towards the *Vitalienbrüder* as the latter supposed. Hitherto, the two cities had taken little action, but the saying 'God's friends and foes of all the world' was presumptuous, to say the least. A permanent solution to the problem of piracy had to be found. Shortly after this report from Bruges, other Flemish cities directed an appeal to the Hanseatic cities whose delegates were meeting in Lübeck, calling on them to take energetic action against the *Vitalienbrüder* and to ban Hamburg and Bremen from trading in stolen goods. Furthermore, the king of England [Richard II] threatened to confiscate Hanseatic property in London to compensate for losses to English shipping. In vain the *Vitalienbrüder* gave assurances that they wished to do no harm to the cities of the Hansa. No longer would Hamburg and Bremen allow them to sell plundered goods in their markets.

THE END OF THE *VITALIENBRÜDER*

The two cities went even further and in 1398 mounted the first ever operation against the *Vitalienbrüder* in the North Sea, which was followed by a larger one in 1400. On 22 April 1400 ships from Hamburg and Lübeck set sail from Hamburg for eastern Friesland. As early as 25 February that

This engraving was once renowned as a portrait of the pirate Klaus Störtebeker. The subject was later revealed to be a courtier of the Emperor Maximilian I, named Kunz von der Rosen.

One of the best-known legends in Germany tells of the execution of Klaus Störtebeker. It is said that his last wish was that those of his comrades whom he could still touch *after* his execution should be spared. His request was granted, and the unbelievable happened: after the executioner had struck off his head, Störtebeker's headless corpse ran off and freed eleven of his companions. But just as he was about to reach the youngest ship's boy, of whom he was especially fond, someone threw a lump of wood between his legs and he fell... In spite of everything, the pirates were all beheaded – thus breaking the Burgomaster's promise, or so the legend has it.

year, Keno tom Brok recognised the gravity of the situation, and together with five other Friesian chieftains, had vowed to refuse refuge to the *Vitalienbrüder*.

The expedition by the Hanseatic fleet was a complete success, as we learn from their ships' captains:

On 22 April we sailed from Hamburg and arrived on 5th May at the western side of the Ems estuary. On the same day we heard that the Vitalienbrüder *were on the eastern side. We dispatched our friends*

thither, and with God's help we swiftly overcame a number of them.
Eighty of them were killed and thrown overboard.
Hanseatic Recessi, I, 4

The East Friesian chieftains, already chastened by the success of the Hansa, were now punished as well. On 6 May the Hanseatic fleet anchored in Emden harbour. Hisko of Emden handed over both the town and its castle to the Hansa and declared himself willing to join in the fight against the *Vitalienbrüder*. On 23 May 1400 all the parishes and chieftains of eastern Friesland signed a written undertaking, that they would no longer grant asylum to the pirates in the territory between the rivers Weser and Ems. Over the 300 or so *Vitalienbrüder* who survived, many fled to Holland or Norway. Those who escaped to Norway were led by Godeke Michels, while those in Holland were commanded – according to written sources – by one Johan Stortebecker. Perhaps this was the famous Klaus Störtebeker, whose name had simply been transcribed incorrectly. If, in fact, they were two different people, the relationship between the two captains has eluded the historical record.

The Hanseatic expedition may have been successful, but the cities of the Hansa probably realised that the problem of piracy had not gone away. Nor could they depend indefinitely on the unstinting support of the East Friesian chieftains. As soon as the Hanseatic ships left Emden, there was reason to fear the return of the *Vitalienbrüder*. On the other hand, the fleet could not be kept in eastern Friesland, allowing the pirates to operate unhindered in the North Sea from bases in the neighbouring but hostile country of Holland. The accuracy of this assessment is demonstrated by the fact that on 11 November 1400 Duke Albrecht of Holland issued letters-of-marque to a gang of *Vitalienbrüder*. Holland was making common cause with the privateers!

On 2 July 1400 the Hanseatic fleet arrived back in Hamburg, in order to be prepared for new missions. However, historical sources tell us practically nothing about the next two years, which were to seal the fate of the pirates.

What is certain is that the *Vitalienbrüder* from Holland, led by their captain, Klaus Störtebeker, returned and established themselves on the island of Heligoland, which was closely allied with the East Friesian chieftains. This meant that that there was the risk of a hostile fleet being permanently based near the mouth of the Elbe and the approaches to Hamburg. The men of Hamburg acted swiftly and decisively. Some time between 15 August and 11 November 1400, a Hamburg fleet under the command of two councillors, Hermann Lange and Nikolaus Schoke, set sail for Heligoland. Of the course of the sea battle we know nothing. There is a legend that the battle was won by Simon of Utrecht on his ship, the *Piebald Cow* – but the vessel of that name was not built until 1401.

It is said that the great *capitaneus* Störtebeker was brought low by treason. The truth is simpler: the Hanseatic fleet was larger. In the Rufus Chronicle from Lübeck we read:

> *In the same year the England-farers from the city of Hamburg fought at sea with the pirates who called themselves* Vitalienbrüder, *and were able to defeat them. Off Heligoland they killed some forty of the pirates and seventy they captured. The latter were taken to Hamburg and all were beheaded; their heads were set up in a meadow beside the Elbe as a sign that they had committed robbery at sea. The captains of these* Vitalienbrüder *were named Wichmann and Klaus Störtebeker.*

Admittedly, the more reliable 'Accounts of the Hamburg Chancery' make no mention of a Klaus Störtebeker, merely of the two Hamburg men who led the naval expedition. Since later accounts mention Godeke Michels several times by name, it is possible that he was the more famous of the two pirate captains. In about 1560, Conrad Tratzinger, professor of law at Rostock and later a syndic of Hamburg, wrote this account of the year 1402:

> *In the following year, which was 1402, the England-farers came upon a number of* Vitalienbrüder *off Heligoland, who were still committing piracy in the western sea. The same had a captain named Clawes Stortebecker [sic] and another named Wichmann. The men of Hamburg attacked the pirates and killed 40 of them; some 70 were taken prisoner and brought to Hamburg, where they were beheaded, as they deserved. Not long afterwards, in the same year, the men of Hamburg captured a further 80* Vitalienbrüder *with their captains, Godeken Michael [sic] and Wigbolden, the latter being a graduate in the liberal arts [promovierter Magister in den freien Künsten]. Thereupon they were taken to Hamburg, there beheaded, and their heads placed with the others on the Grasbrook meadow.*

Historical research has since revised the date of the naval expedition, given here as 1402, to 1400. The operation in that year was over in a few days. The pirates were not given the benefit of a formal trial; the executions took place very soon after the arrival of the prisoners in Hamburg.

Godeke Michels, who had returned in 1401 from Norway to eastern Friesland – almost certainly at the behest of the Dutch Duke Albrecht – was overpowered in the Weser with his last few ships, and executed shortly afterwards. In a document dated 27 April 1402, we read:

> We wish to remind you, dear friends, that Godeke Michels and his henchmen, other Vitalienbrüder, were at sea and that we equipped our own men, who overcame the said Godeke Michels and his henchmen, together with their cog.
> Hanseatic Recessi, I, 5

The rest is legend. The *Vitalienbrüder* disappeared from history, and not a few of their ships lie at the bottom of the Baltic and the North Sea.

11 THE MARITIME HERITAGE OF THE BALTIC AND THE NORTH SEA

160

THE MARITIME

HERITAGE OF

THE BALTIC

AND THE

NORTH SEA

If today you ask tourists from inland about the maritime heritage of northern Europe's past, you can be sure that most of them will reply: preserved sailing ships, floating museums of old ships and old fishing boats. In every port city there are 'historic ships' and associated memorabilia to be seen. We also have vivid images of Viking ships and their marauding raids, as well as the cogs, those symbols of the Hanseatic age.

But there is more to the maritime heritage than this. The landscape of marine culture is created above and below the surface by traditional sea routes, harbours and their related infrastructure. The maritime heritage embraces ports, shipping channels, canals, navigation marks, lighthouses, pilot-stations, fishing ports, boatyards, wrecks and place-names associated with the sea. These elements have not always been preserved, but the combination of these groups of monuments reveals structures before our eyes. We see fishing and seaborne trade as part of the economic landscape. Even religious notions of the sea have left traces behind. This is impressively demonstrated by the Viking-age burials in boat-graves, pictorial stones and grave-fields in which stones are laid out in the shape of ships. After the Middle Ages ships were often depicted on the tombstones of sea captains, and we even find these in churches.

In the area immediately adjoining the shore we find the paraphernalia of fishing and of boatbuilding and shipbuilding. This landscape can best be understood by viewing it from the sea, with the eyes of the seaman. The means of transport in this zone are river-borne and coastal vessels, as well as deep-water shipping. Not only the coastal areas but also rivers and larger lakes are part of the maritime environment. Further inland lies a region that is predominantly agricultural but which once profited from seaborne trade and supplied the trading towns with farm produce and raw materials, such as timber for shipbuilding.

If we are to understand the cultural heritage of this landscape, we must look simultaneously at the evolution of ships and the related infrastructure ashore. Admittedly, this is not possible for all coastal regions in equal measure. For example, the intensive modern development of the southern Baltic coast and the transformation of the coastline have wiped out most traces of early medieval culture. Some of its relics now lie at the bottom of the sea. Hence, it is precisely these remains that are of particular significance for the reconstruction of the landscape of maritime culture.

161

THE MARITIME
HERITAGE OF
THE BALTIC
AND THE
NORTH SEA

The little graveyard of Mårup church on the shores of the Jammerbucht ('Bay of Sorrows') in northern Jutland bears witness to the many shipwrecks and men who drowned. Ominously, outside the church, stands the anchor of the British frigate *Crescent*, which went down in 1808. The ship was driven by an onshore wind – just as the German seamen's handbook would warn in 1927 – and came too close to the hazardous coast with its breakers and sandbanks. The crew attempted to throw out the anchors and prevent the ship from being smashed. When, 17 hours later, the last anchor had dragged loose, the frigate duly broke up in the raging sea and 226 sailors, including some wives and children who were aboard, lost their lives. Only 55 were rescued.

When we consider the coastal landscape and the sea routes from the Viking age up to the late Middle Ages, we realise what a unique cultural heritage northern Europe possesses. And the medieval maritime heritage is visible today in the buildings of Hanseatic cities like Lübeck. On the other hand, many former entrepôts and trading settlements, such as Langwurten on the North Sea, have forfeited their maritime function and undergone a transformation into rural communities.

Archaeological excavations expose buried culture of this kind and thus open a window on the past. At the same time, marine archaeology extends from underwater research on wrecks to the exploration of shipping routes, of the early trading settlements and the evolution of a maritime culture in coastal regions. This archaeological knowledge complements historical research – the analysis of written and pictorial sources.

Maritime culture, seafaring and distant lands exert a fascination to this day, and initiatives by the Council of Europe and the European Union, such as the 'European Landscape Convention', emphasise the value of cultural landscapes and thus of maritime regions. In 1997 the Ministers of the Environment from three North Sea countries (Germany, Denmark and the Netherlands) met to launch the EU project entitled 'Landscape and Cultural Heritage of the Wadden Sea' – the unique combination of islands, creeks, sandbanks and saltmarshes that stretches from northern Holland to the west coast of Jutland. Originally, the project had been limited to ecological questions but, following local protests, the ministers agreed to assign the same value and importance to the *cultural* heritage of this coastline as to its natural heritage. The EU made available a grant of 1 million Euros for the mapping of the region's cultural heritage. The resulting report can be found on the *Lancewad* website.

Although the UK was not involved in the Wadden Sea project, there are comparable projects under way in Britain, such as the Great Estuary Partnership covering the Kent and Essex shores of the Thames estuary, and English Heritage's Historic Landscape Programme. The Humber Area Wetland Project is producing cultural maps of that area.

For the purposes of another programme, the EU project *Navis 1,* a number of museums have joined forces: the Museum of Ancient Shipping in the Central Romano-Germanic Museum, Mainz, the Centre for Maritime Archaeology at the National Museum, Copenhagen, the National Museum of Ship Archaeology at Ketelhaven in the Netherlands, as well as the Shipwreck Heritage Centre in Hastings, Kent, and the Guernsey Museum and Galleries in the Channel Islands. They have jointly set up a database of historical ships from Roman times to the Middle Ages, which is accessible to the general public. It can be reached via the website of the Romano-Germanic Museum (Römisch-Germanisches Zentralmuseum) in Mainz. The German Shipping Museum and the Museum of Underwater Archaeology in Sassnitz, and the Haithabu Museum in Hedeby, Germany also have exhibits of maritime heritage.

The present-day development of the coastal regions of the North Sea and the Baltic is founded on this heritage, and we should do everything we can to preserve it and make sustainable use of it. Without the courage and daring of seamen Europe would be much the poorer.

162

THE MARITIME

HERITAGE OF

THE BALTIC

AND THE

NORTH SEA

GLOSSARY

Adam of Bremen: A canon of Bremen cathedral and head of the monastery school. Born probably before 1050, he died some time between 1081 and 1085, and was originally from Upper (i.e. central or southern) Germany. His best-known work is the *Gesta Hammaburgensis ecclesiae pontificum,* four books on the history of the archbishopric of Hamburg and the islands of the North Sea.

Ahmed Ibn Fadlan: An Arab envoy of the Caliph of Baghdad. In the tenth century he made contact with the Bulgars living on the banks of the Volga and the peoples of Kievan Rus. These people traded with the Arab world, selling furs and slaves in exchange for silver. In 922 Ibn Fadlan wrote an account of his journey (*Al-Risalab*).

Almere: Name given in Roman times to the Dutch inland sea, which later became the Zuider Zee, when the waters of North Sea broke into it. In the 1920s and 1930s it was dammed and partially drained, to form the Ijsselmeer.

Angles: A Germanic tribe, which originally came from present-day Schleswig-Holstein and Denmark. Today the region between the Flensburg Fjord and the Schlei Fjord is still called 'Angeln'.

Anglo-Saxon Chronicle: Around 892 the Anglo-Saxon king, Alfred the Great, commissioned a record of the most important historical events in his realm. This chronicle was continued by different scholars into the twelfth century.

Astrolabe: Apparatus for making astronomical, astrological and geographical measurements; invented by the Arabs, it was in use until the seventeenth century.

Beowulf: tenth-century Anglo-Saxon epic poem about a hero of the same name.

Bowsprit: Wooden spar projecting beyond the bow of a sailing ship, which carries the foresail or jib.

Byzantium: The original Greek name for the city on the Bosphorus, which was renamed Constantinople in honour of the later Roman emperor, Constantine. After the fall of the western Roman empire, the Greek-speaking eastern empire reverted to the old name. It was capital of the Byzantine empire until it finally fell to the Turks in 1453 and is now known as Istanbul.

Caravel: A relatively sophisticated sailing vessel that probably originated in Portugal and was introduced into northern Europe in the sixteenth century. It had three masts and some fore-and-aft sails. The term 'carvel-built', where the planks are laid edge to edge, is derived from 'caravel'.

Carrack: In medieval times the name 'hulk' (from the German *Holk*) was usually given to this type of vessel, though 'carrack' became more usual, while 'hulk' (q.v.) has different connotations. The carrack replaced the cog (q.v.) at the beginning of the fifteenth century, and is characterised by the superstructures or 'castles' in the bow and stern. It had a keel and a rounded hull, with planking that swept up almost vertically at the bow and stern. Columbus's *Santa Maria* was an example of this type of vessel.

Cog: Typical sailing cargo ship of the thirteenth century, it had a flat bottom and high, wall-like sides, sloping stem and stern-posts and a stern rudder. Though clinker-built, the overlapping of the planks was often reversed, i.e. each lower plank overlapped the one above. It had a single, central mast and a square sail suspended from a yard-arm. The cog was the predominant form of seagoing vessel in northern Europe and further afield until about 1400.

Courland (German: *Kurland*) Historically a German-speaking and German-owned territory on the Baltic coast in what is now Latvia, subjugated and Christianised in the thirteenth century by the Teutonic Knights.

Denarius: Silver coin of the Frankish empire.

Dendrochronology: Method of dating ancient pieces of wood using the rings added to a tree's circumference each year. Variations in summer temperature and rainfall in a particular region create a pattern in the rings. By matching the pattern with that of other finds already dated, a date-range can be established for every new find.

Dollart: In a storm-surge in the late Middle Ages the sea inundated a large area of land around the estuary of the river Ems, in north-west Germany, creating what is now called the Dollart Bight.

Finno-Ugrian: Racial and linguistic group that originated some 7,000 years ago in the northern Urals and migrated westward, now occupying Karelia (NW Russia), Estonia, Finland, northern Sweden and northern Norway (see also Sami).

Freeboard: The height of a ship from the waterline to the top of its side, or main deck.

German Bight: A large area of the North Sea bounded by Schleswig-Holstein in the east and the north-west coast of Germany to the south. Its western extremity is longitude 5 degrees east.

Gotland Association: Association of German merchants who visited Gotland regularly for trading purposes and maintained offices (*Kontore*) there. In Latin sources: *universi mercatores Imperii Romani* [Holy Roman Empire, q.v.] *Gotlandiam frequentantes*

Greifswald: River port near the Baltic coast of Germany.

Harald Hardrada: King of Norway, who invaded Britain in September of 1066. Harald and his ally Tostig, the exiled Earl of Northumbria, were defeated and killed by King Harold of England at the Battle of Stamford Bridge.

Hedeby /Haithabu: Hedeby is the Danish name, Haithabu the Old German, for an early medieval trading settlement on the east coast of Schleswig-Holstein. It was later supplanted by the port of Schleswig. Hedeby has been the subject of various archaeological excavations since the 1930s. The semicircular defensive wall that once protected the settlement can still be clearly seen.

Heligoland (German: *Helgoland*)**:** A flat-topped island of rock in the North Sea, some 65 km north-west of the mouth of the Elbe.

Holy Roman Empire: When the Roman Empire, which had officially adopted Christianity in the fourth century AD, fell to the invading barbarians a century later, the flame of Christianity was kept alive and, eventually, in 800, Pope Leo III crowned Charlemagne emperor, since there had been a split with the Byzantine emperor in the east. This was not, however, the inauguration of the Holy Roman Empire as such. That did not take place until Otto I of Saxony (reigned 963–973) was crowned emperor of Rome in 962. This title was handed on through the Saxon, Salian, Hohenstaufen and Habsburg dynasties until the late eighteenth century. The Holy Roman Empire was predominantly a German entity, which exercised certain powers, mainly judicial, over the numerous kingdoms, principalities and dukedoms of German-speaking Europe. If a city became a Free Imperial City, it enjoyed great privileges and was subject to no feudal ruler.

Hulk: from German *Holk*. The medieval name for what is more usually called a 'carrack'; a flat-bottomed wooden vessel used as a cargo ship from AD 800 off the Friesian coast of the North Sea. In the High Middle Ages it developed and further supplanted the cog (q.v.).

Ibn Fadlan (*see* Ahmed Ibn Fadlan)

Ibrahim Ibn Yakoub at-Tartoushi: A Jewish traveller from Moorish Spain, who was sent by the Caliph of Cordoba in 963 on a mission to the court of the German king, Otto I, who had been crowned Holy Roman Emperor in 962. His account was passed on by later geographers.

Jutes: A Germanic tribe, which originally inhabited Jutland and Schleswig-Holstein. During the great migrations of the fourth and fifth centuries AD, the Jutes were among the Germanic tribes who occupied England.

Kaperbrief (German): Similar to a 'letter of marque' in England. In the Middle Ages, if someone had a legal claim against a ship-owner, he was issued a *Kaperbrief* by his city or feudal overlord. This was an entitlement to seize a ship and obtain compensation by taking its cargo. It was frequently used as a means of legitimising piracy.

Keelson: A baulk of timber laid on top of the keel to increase its strength.

Kontor (plural ***Kontore, Kontoren***): Historical German term for commercial premises including both storehouse and counting-house or business office. In certain major ports outside Germany, merchants would establish a joint *Kontor*, such as the Stalhof (Steelyard) in London.

Kven: An early Finnish-speaking Scandinavian tribe who occupied the coasts of the White Sea and northern Norway.

Ladby: Village on the north coast of the Danish island of Fyn.

Leeboards: Lateral boards on some shallow-draught wooden vessels, which can be raised and lowered by rotation. When lowered on the side opposite to the direction of the wind (lee side), they provided added lateral stability. They can still be seen on Thames sailing-barges and Dutch barge-yachts.

Merovingian (dynasty): The Merovingians were a dynasty of Frankish kings who ruled, between the fifth and eight centuries, over a highly fluid territory in parts of what are now France and Germany.

Nautical mile: Measurement of distance at sea, or in the air, defined as the distance between each minute of latitude at the equator (i.e. 1:21,600 of the earth's circumference, or 1,852 metres).

Obodrites (also Abodrites): A West Slavic race who settled in western Mecklenburg and eastern Holstein in the seventh century AD. They had contacts with the Franks, Saxons and Danes. Their ruling princes adopted Christianity and invited German settlers into their territory, which corresponded roughly to the modern German province of Mecklenburg.

Orosius (Paulus) (c. 385–c. 420): A Spanish-born priest and writer of a history of the world. In the ninth century the English king, Alfred the Great, translated the work into Anglo-Saxon and added to it two contemporary travel accounts (see Ottar and Wulfstan).

Ottar: A Norwegian landowner and travelling merchant, who in 890 sailed beyond the Arctic Circle and into the White Sea. An account of his voyage was translated into Anglo-Saxon and appended to Orosius' history of the world.

Pram: Historically, a small, shallow-draught workboat, usually with a square bow. The term 'pram dinghy' is still used by yachtsmen.

Runic: A Scandinavian alphabet first recorded in the third century AD, which was also used in the British Isles. The Icelandic sagas tell that the Runic script was invented by the god Odin, which suggests that it was the first written form of language in that region.

Sami: The now accepted name for the nomadic tribes of northern Scandinavia, also known as Lapps or Lapplanders.

Sceattas: Originally Anglo-Saxon coins, copies were also minted by the Friesians and Danes.

Schnigge (German): A small, manoeuvrable, shallow-draught sailing vessel.

Schute (Flemish): A sailing vessel for carrying cargoes on inland waters, probably similar to a Norfolk wherry.

Skerry: From a Norse word (cf. modern Swedish *skär*), meaning a rocky islet off the mainland. Clustered skerries are found off the coasts of Norway, Sweden, Finland, the west of Scotland and the west of Ireland.

Summarium Henrici: An alphabetical reference book written in Latin, which was probably compiled in either the eleventh or thirteenth centuries.

Terra sigillata: Form of highly prized Roman pottery.

Trientes: Gold coins of the Merovingian era.

Wends, Wendish: General terms used to describe the pagan Slavic tribes on the north-eastern borders of the German Empire.

Wolin: Now a small Baltic coastal town in Poland situated at the point where the inland sea called the Zalew Szczecinski (German: Stettiner Haff) is linked to the Baltic by the Dzwina channel. Called Wollin by German-speakers, Domsborg by the Danes and Vineta by some medieval historians and geographers, it was founded in the eighth or ninth century AD and grew to be the most important trading port on the Baltic. In 1098 it was attacked by the Danes, and was destroyed in further campaigns during the twelfth century.

Wulfstan: A seafarer of unknown origin, perhaps Anglo-Saxon or Norman, whose principal voyages were along the southern coast of the Baltic. An account of his voyage from Hedeby to Truso, near modern Gdansk, was appended to the Anglo-Saxon translation of Orosius' history of the world.

Wurt (German): In Dutch, German and Danish coastal areas, an artificially created, elongated hill on which a settlement has been built, secure from flooding and, to some extent, from attack.

FURTHER READING

Adam von Bremen, *Gesta Hammburgensis ecclesiae pontificum. Geschichte der Erzbischöfe von Hamburg* (ed. A. Heine). Historiker des Deutschen Altertums (Essen 1986)

Ambrosiani, B., 'Birka, Its Waterways and Hinterland', in Crumlin-Pedersen (1991), 99–104

   and Clarke, H. (eds), *Investigations into the Black Earth*. Birka Studies 1 (Stockholm 1992)

Arbman, H., *The Vikings* (London 1961)

Austin, D. and Alcock, L. (eds), *From the Baltic to the Black Seas. Studies in Medieval Archaeology* (London 1990)

Batey, C.E. *et al.* (eds), *The Viking Age in Caithness, Orkney and the Northern Atlantic* (Edinburgh 1993)

Bazelmans, J., 'Beowulf, A Man of Worth', in Tyne and Wear Museum (ed.), *Kings of the North Sea AD 250–850* (Newcastle upon Tyne 2000), 33–40

Bergersen, R., *Vinland Bibliographie. Writings relating to the Norse in Greenland and America* (Tromsoe 1997)

Berggren, L. (ed.), *Cogs, Cargoes and Commerce. Maritime Bulk Trade in Northern Europe 1150–1400* (Toronto 2002)

Bigelow, G.F. (ed.), *The Norse in the North Atlantic*. Acta Archaeologica 61 (Copenhagen 1990)

Bill, J., *NAVIS 1 – A Cooperative Project in Maritime Archaeology*, supported by the EAND Maritime Archaeology Newsletter from Roskilde, Denmark 8 (1997), 15–16

Bowes, D.R., *The Natural Environment of the Inner Hebrides* (Edinburgh 1981)

Brisbane, M. (ed.), *The Archaeology of Novgorod, Russia* (Woodbridge 1992)

Bruce-Mitford, R., *The Sutton Hoo Ship-Burial* 1 (London 1975)

Callmer, J., 'Urbanization in Scandinavia and the Baltic Region c AD 700–1100. Trading Places, Centres and Early Urban Sites', in Ambrosiani, B. and Clarke, H. (eds), *Developments Around the Baltic Sea in the Viking Age*. Birka Studies III (Birka 1994), 50–70

Campbell, J.G., *The Anglo-Saxons* (London 1982)

Viking Artefacts. A Select Catalogue (London 1980)

The Viking World (London 1989)

and Kidd, D., *The Vikings* (London 1980)

Carver, M., *Sutton Hoo. A Seventh-century Princely Burial Ground and its Context* (London 2005)

(ed.), *The Cross goes North. Processes of Conversion in Northern Europe AD 300–1300.* (York 2003)

Council of Europe, *European Landscape Convention*. European Treaty Series 176 (Bruxelles 2000)

Crumlin-Pedersen, O. (ed.), *Aspects of Maritime Scandinavia AD 200–1200*. Proceedings of the Nordic Seminar on Maritime Aspects of Archaeology, 13–15 March 1989 (Roskilde 1991)

and Munch Thye, B. (eds), *The Ship as a Symbol in Prehistoric and Medieval Scandinavia*. Publications of the National Museum. Studies in Archaeology and History 1 (Copenhagen 1995)

and Rieck, F., 'The Nydam Ships. Old and New Investigations at a Classic Site', in Coles, J., Fenwick, V. and Hutchinson, G. (eds), *A Spirit of Enquiry. Essays for Ted Wright* (Exeter 1993)

Fudge, J., *Cargoes, Embargoes and Emissaries. The Commericial and Poltical Interaction of England and the German Hanse 1450–1510* (Toronto 1995)

Gräslund, A.-S., *The Burial Customs. A Study of the Graves on Björkö.* Birka IV (Stockholm 1980)

Gulløv, H.C. *From Middle Ages to Colonial Times. Archaeological and Ethnohistorical Studies of the Thule Culture in South West Greenland 1300–1800 AD*. Meddelser om Grønland, Man & Society 23 (Copenhagen 1997)

Hall, R.A., *The Viking Dig. The Excavations in York* (York 1984)

Viking Age Archaeology in Britain and Ireland (Princes Risborough 1990)

Hannestadt, K. *et al.* (eds), *Varangian Problems*. Scando-Slavica. Supplementum 1 (Copenhagen 1970)

Hastrup, K., *Culture and History in Medieval Iceland. An Anthropological Analysis of Structure and Change* (Oxford 1985)

Hedeager, L., *Iron-Age Societies. From Tribe to State in Northern Europe 500 BC to AD 700* (Oxford/Cambridge 1992)

Heidinga, H.A., *Frisia in the First Millennium. An Outline* (Utrecht 1997)

Herrmann, J., 'The Northern Slavs', in Wilson, D.M. (ed.), *The Northern World* (London 1980)

Holmquist, W., *Germanic Art during the First Millennium AD* (Stockholm 1955)

Hudson, B.T., *Viking Pirates and Christian Princes. Dynasty, Religion, and Empire in the North Atlantic* (Oxford 2005)

Ingstad, H., *The Norse Discovery of America 2: The Historical Background and Evidence of the Norse Settlement Discovered in Newfoundland* (Oslo 1985)

and Ingstad, A.S., *The Norse Discovery of America: The Excavation of a Norse Settlement at L'Anse aux Meadows, Newfoundland 1961–1968* (Oslo 1977, rev. 1985)

Jansson, I., 'Communications between Scandinavia and Eastern Europe in the Viking Age', in Düwel, K. (ed.), *Untersuchungen zu Handel und Verkehr der vor- und frühgeschichtlichen Zeit* 4 (Göttingen 1987)

Jensen, S., *The Vikings of Ribe* (Ribe 1991)

Jones, G., *A History of the Vikings* (Oxford/New York 1984)

Keller, Chr., *The Eastern Settlement Reconsidered. Some Analyses of Norse Medieval Greenland.* 2 parts (Oslo 1989)

Kendall, C.B. and Wells, P.S. (eds), *Voyage to the Other World. The Legacy of Sutton Hoo* (Minneapolis 1992)

King Alfred's Orosius (ed. H. Sweet), Early English Text Society 79 (London 1883)

Kinvig, H.R. *The Isle of Man. A Social, Cultural and Political History* (no place 1975)

Kivikari, O., *The Legacy of Hansa, the Baltic Economic Region* (Helsinki 1996)

Krogh, K., *Viking Greenland* (Copenhagen 1967)

Lacy, T., *Ring of Seasons. Iceland – Its Culture and History* (Ann Arbor 1998)

Lengsfeld, K. and Meier, D., 'Livestock and Trade. The Landscape of Schleswig-Holstein's West Coast in the First Millenium AD', in Tyne and Wear Museum (ed.), *Kings of the North Sea AD 250–850* (Newcastle upon Tyne 2000), 133–42

Lindquist, S.O. (ed.), *Society and Trade in the Baltic during the Viking Age* (Visby 1985)

Loyd, T.H., *England and the German Hanse 1157–1611. A Study of Trade and Commercial Diplomacy* (Cambridge 1991)

Loyn, H.R., *The Vikings in Wales* (London 1976)

Lund, N. (ed.), *Two Voyagers at the Court of King Alfred* (York 1984)

Magnusson, M., *Vikings!* (London 1980)

McKitterick, R., *The Frankish Kingdoms under the Carolingians 751–987* (London 1983)

Meier, D., *Bauer, Bürger, Edelmann. Stadt und Land im Mittelalter* (Ostfildern 2003)

'Beispiele interdisziplinärer genetischer Siedlungsforschung in Skandinavien. Stand der Forschung und europäische Perspektiven. Siedlungsforschung', *Archäologie–Geschichte–Geographie* 18 (2000), 101–8

Landschaftsentwicklung und Siedlungsgeschichte des Eiderstedter und Dithmarscher Küstengebietes als Teilregionen des Nordseegebietes. Teil 1 Die Siedlungen; Teil 2 Der Siedlungsraum. Untersuchungen der AG Küstenarchäologie des FTZ-Westküste. Universitätsforschungen zur Prähistorischen Archäologie 79 (Bonn 2001)

*Siedeln und Leben am Rande des Meeres. Von der Steinzeit bis in das Mitt*elalter (Stuttgart 2003)

Millard, A., *Eric the Red. The Vikings Sail the Atlantic* (London 1993)

Musset, Lucien, *The Bayeux Tapestry*, trans. Richard Rex (Woodbridge 2005)

Myhre, B., *'Boathouses as Indicators of Political Organisation'*, Norwegian Archaeological Review *18 (1985), 36–60*

Noomann, T.S., 'The Vikings and Russia. Some New Directions and Approaches to an Old Problem', in Samson, R. (ed.), *Social Approaches to Viking Studies* (Glasgow 1991)

Olsen, O. and Crumlin-Pedersen, O., *Five Viking Ships from Roskilde Fjord* (Copenhagen 1978)

Olsen, O., Skanby-Madsen, J. and Rieck, F. (eds), *Shipshape. Essays for Ole Crumlin-Pedersen* (Roskilde 1995)

Randsborg, K., *Hjortspring. Warfare and Sacrifice in Early Europe* (Aarhus 1995)

The Viking Age in Denmark (London 1980)

Reinders, R., *Shipwrecks of the Zuiderzee*. Flevobericht 197 (Lelystad 1982)

Rieck, F., 'The Institute of Maritime Archaeology, The Beginning of Maritime Research in Denmark', in Olsen, J., Skamby-Madsen, J. and Rieck, F. (eds), *Shipshape. Essays for Ole Crumlin* (Roskilde 1995), 19–36

Roesdahl, E., *The Vikings* (London 1992)

Viking Age Denmark (London 1982)

and Wilson, D.M. (eds), *From Viking to Crusader. Scandinavia and Europe AD 700–1100* (London/New York 1982)

Stenberger, M., *Sweden* (London/New York 1963)

Sveinbjarnadottir, G., *Form Abandonment in Medieval and Post-Medieval Iceland. An Interdisciplinary Study*. Oxbow Monograph 17 (Oxdord 1992)

Tyne and Wear Museum (ed.), *Kings of the North Sea AD 250–850* (Newcastle upon Tyne 2000)

Vebaek, C.C., *Narsaq – A Norse Landname Farm* (Copenhagen 1993)

Vollmer, M., Gudberg, M., Maluck, M., Marrewijk, D. van and Schlicksbier, G., *LANCEWAD. Landscape and Cultural Heritage of the Wadden Sea Region*. Wadden Sea Ecosystem No. 12 (Wilhelmshaven 2001)

Wallace, B.L., 'The Vikings in North America, Myth and Reality', in Samson, R. (ed.), *Social Approaches to Viking Studies* (Glasgow 1991)

Wallace, P., *The Viking Age Buildings of Dublin* (Dublin 1983)

Westerdahl, Chr., 'The Maritime Cultural Landscape', *The International Journal of Nautical Archaeology* 21/1 (1992), 5–14

Whitelock, D. (ed.), *English Historical Documents c. 500–1042* (London 1979)

Willis, Lionel, *The Coastal Trade* (London 1975)

Wilson, D.H., *The Bayeux Tapestry* (London 2004)

Wilson, D.M. (ed.), *The Northern World, The History and Heritage of Northern Europe AD 400–1100* (London 1980)

Zimmern, H., *The Hansa Towns* (Reprint, New York/London 1907)

173

FURTHER

READING

SOURCES OF ILLUSTRATIONS

INDEX

Numbers in **bold** indicate an illustration or map on that page